ISBN 978-1-331-56569-7
PIBN 10206649

This book is a reproduction of an important historical work. Forgotten Books uses
state-of-the-art technology to digitally reconstruct the work, preserving the original format
whilst repairing imperfections present in the aged copy. In rare cases, an imperfection in
the original, such as a blemish or missing page, may be replicated in our edition. We do,
however, repair the vast majority of imperfections successfully; any imperfections that
remain are intentionally left to preserve the state of such historical works.

Similar Books Are Available from
www.forgottenbooks.com

MASTER OF BALLIOL

BY THE HON.

LIONEL A. TOLLEMACHE

AUTHOR OF 'SAFE STUDIES,' ETC.

EDWARD ARNOLD

Publisher to the India Office

LONDON
37 BEDFORD STREET

NEW YORK
70 FIFTH AVENUE

PREFACE.

THESE Recollections, which first appeared in the *Journal of Education* for May, 1895, are now republished with considerable additions.

It may be at first thought that my record of Jowett's opinions is too often diluted with the addition of opinions of my own. It should, however, be remembered that I have always accounted myself one of his disciples. It is, therefore, perhaps not wholly irrelevant to give expression to some of my opinions, in the formation of which I have been, directly or indirectly, conscious of his influence. In such cases my own views are in some measure the outcome of his teaching; and thus they may be said to represent his views at second-hand, or, at any rate, his views with a difference. *By their fruits ye shall know them.*

BENJAMIN JOWETT, D.D.,

MASTER OF BALLIOL.

I.

'I cannot hide that some have striven,
Achieving calm, to whom was given
The joy that mixes man with heaven.

Who, rowing hard against the stream,
Saw distant gates of Eden gleam,
And did not dream it was a dream ;

*   *   *   *

Which did accomplish their desire,
Bore and forebore, and did not tire,
Like Stephen, an unquenched fire.'

TENNYSON.

WHEN I went up to Balliol in 1856, I became a pupil of Jowett. The class which I obtained in 1860 was in the main due to his assiduous and discerning care. He helped me both directly and indirectly. 'Little time is lost through ill-health,' he once said to me, 'though much is lost through idleness.' Doubtless this was an exaggeration, but it was the sort of friendly exaggeration which stimulated me to

struggle against physical disadvantages. Nor did
the stimulus which he thus applied bring with it a
sense of irritation. The despotic side of his character, of which some of his pupils complained,
seldom or never showed itself in my presence—at
any rate, in relation to myself. On the contrary,
when beset by trials and difficulties, I found him
generally a wise and always a sympathetic coun-
sellor. And thus it was that, though I am not
given to the expression of strong emotion, yet, when
in 1893 the news reached me of the sad event which
deprived me of my oldest and truest friend and
Oxford of her brightest ornament, the words rose
unbidden to my lips, 'I feel that there has gone
a glory from the earth.'

I will begin with a few of my early recollections of
Jowett, reserving to a later stage those of his early
sayings which have a special bearing on my estimate
of his character. It is necessary, however, to note
one circumstance which renders every written
account of him incomplete. *The voice was the man.*
To say this of Jowett is a pardonable exaggeration,
and is at once felt to be so if we observe how in-
evitably his friends, when repeating his sayings, fall
into his peculiar accent. Would that his cherubic
chirp (so to call it), when he was at his ease and at
his best, had been embalmed in a phonograph—
embalmed so as to be a *vox verisimilis*, though, alas,
a *vox et præterea nihil!* Let me add that his
peculiar charm, a charm springing in great part

from incongruity, was brought home to one whenever one saw him ('O qualis facies et quali digna
tabellâ'), with his commanding forehead and his
infantine smile; but especially was it brought home
to one when one heard him giving utterance to
genially cynical sentiments in his pleasantly falsetto
voice.

In consequence of my evangelical training, I fell
under his influence with extreme reluctance; for I
firmly believed that his pupils ran great risk of
becoming strangers to the household of faith, and of
denying the Lord that bought them. Yet I could
not help cross-questioning him. One remark, in
particular, which I drew from him gave me a great
shock. He was in favour of the right of divorce,
and I asked him how he reconciled that right with
certain passages in the Gospels. He turned suddenly round, and asked: 'What do you make of the
text, "Swear not at all"?' 'Does not this text
apply to profane swearing?' 'No,' was his short
answer. His point obviously was that, as we
habitually disregard one plain utterance of Christ,
why may we not disregard another? I was not
prepared for this reasoning, and its immediate effect
on me was to make me feel scruples about taking
judicial oaths.

Jowett perceived that a belief in eternal torment,
as taught by my early pastors and masters, had
made a great impression on me. He remarked that
this belief, when fully realized, becomes insupport-
able; and he added that Dr. Pusey had once

preached on the subject with so much energy that some of the congregation had to leave the church.

I asked him whether, when John the Baptist said, ' He that hath two coats, let him impart to him that hath none; and he that hath meat, let him do likewise,' the command was not meant to be taken literally; if the Baptist had merely been giving utterance to an Oriental hyperbole, he would hardly have gone out of his way to add the clause about the meat. Wishing to allay my scrupulousness, Jowett laughingly exclaimed: ' This is just the sort of remark that I should have expected to find in an Alexandrian commentator.' But in saying this he was, perhaps unconsciously, veiling his real opinion; for long afterwards, when I had been weaned from my early Bibliolatry, he said to me : ' There seems to me to be much more in the New Testament in praise of poverty than we like to acknowledge.'

When I had become thoroughly his disciple, [I once called his attention to the strange shifts to which moral progress reduced some of the prophets in their dealings with the barbarous portions of the Mosaic law; insomuch that one of them declared that God had given to His people statutes that were not good. Jowett replied that the strongest passage of the sort was that in which Jeremiah (vii. 22) represents God as disclaiming the authorship of the entire Ceremonial Law: ' I spake not unto your fathers nor commanded them in the day that I brought them out of the land of Egypt, concerning burnt offerings or sacrifices.'

I asked Jowett whether too much importance is not attached to the rule of criticism, that, where there are two readings, the worse, or at any rate the less obvious of them, is to be preferred; may not textual errors have arisen as often from the negligence of copyists as from their misplaced zeal? He replied that he agreed with me; but it seemed to him to be a safe rule that, where there are various readings in the New Testament, the least orthodox of them ought to be preferred. He doubtless thought that the early Christian copyists did not often err through lack of care; while, on the other hand, familiar examples tend to show that the besetting sin of those copyists was pious disingenuousness.

I inquired what sort of efficacy he attributed to Baptism. 'Surely,' he replied, 'you and I are the better for having been born and brought up in the Christian fellowship; and Baptism is the sign of that fellowship.'

T.—'But suppose the case of an infant dying before Baptism, or of a person who, through some negligence of the priest, has not been duly baptized, but who passes through life believing that he has been duly baptized. Surely the Catholic doctrine is, or used to be, that such a person is in peril of being damned.'

J.—'That is a revolting doctrine. The Fathers thought it, though.'

George Sand has declared the practice of praying for temporal blessings to be 'sheer idolatry.' Jowett went so far in this direction as to affirm the practice to be a superstition. But he thought that prayers for spiritual blessings may have an objective as well as a subjective effect—may have, that is, an effect which is not dependent on the nervous condition of him who prays and who expects his prayers to be answered.

I asked him whether he did not think that St. Paul was referring to the entire Israelite nation when he said : ' My heart's desire and prayer to God for Israel is that they might be saved.' If so, it seems to follow that, when he goes on to say that all Israel shall be saved, he means to affirm that all persons of Hebrew descent will go to heaven. Jowett agreed with me in thinking that St. Paul was speaking of the Hebrew nation ; but it seemed to him that the words ' shall be saved ' may mean ' shall be restored to Palestine.'

It must (I may note in passing) have been after pondering on this embarrassing text that the youthful Bunyan began to scrutinize his own pedigree in the manner (somewhat unsympathetically) mentioned by Macaulay : ' At one time he took it into his head that all persons of Israelite blood would be saved, and tried to make out that he partook of that blood ; but his hopes were speedily destroyed by his father, who seems to have had no ambition to be regarded as a Jew.'

Jowett went on to say that St. Paul inclined to Universalism in the text, ' God hath concluded them all in unbelief that he might have mercy upon them all.' ' But would he,' I asked, ' have extended this hope to Elymas the sorcerer and Alexander the coppersmith?' Jowett intimated that the Apostle's verdict on such men would have depended on the frame of mind in which he happened to be, and he characteristically added · 'I doubt whether, when the Jews sought to slay him, he would have said : "All Israel shall be saved."' This was certainly a view of inspiration very different from that in which I had been brought up.

I asked him whether it was not certain that the Scarlet Woman in the Apocalypse was meant to designate Pagan Rome. He surprised me by answering that the city represented was a mystical compound of Babylon, Rome, and Jerusalem ('where also our Lord was crucified'—Rev. xi. 8).

On my inquiring whether he attached great historical value to the fourth Gospel, he replied that it was incredible that Christ should, during long conversations occurring at different dates, have habitually spoken in the style attributed to him by the Synoptists, and should also have habitually spoken in the very different style attributed to him by the fourth Evangelist.

In my undergraduate days I drew from him the admission that he disbelieved in the story of Jonah and the Whale, but that he kept his judgment in suspense as to whether the Law had or had not been given from Sinai. He told me at the same time that, even when he had felt most sceptical, his belief in immortality had never wavered. It may serve to mark the difference between a Platonist's and an Aristotelian's point of view if I mention that, on my speaking of this unfaltering conviction of his to Charles Austin, the latter dryly remarked : ' If I had that conviction, I could believe all the rest.'

It will be gathered from the foregoing examples that I was in the habit of cross-examining Jowett freely, and that he bore the cross-examination with admirable patience. Once, however, when towards the end of a walk I proposed launching out on a new topic of discussion, he laughingly protested : ' I must make a bargain with you that, when we take a walk together, you don't put more than one of your stodgy questions !'

From these theological utterances of his I pass on to his views on matters connected, in some instances, with University studies.

He complained to me long ago that greater academical results had not been obtained from the ablest of the wealthy undergraduates of Christ Church. On those favourites of Nature and Fortune the stimulus of ambition might, he thought, be made to act powerfully, if only it were skilfully applied. This recalls what he once said to a pupil : ' Young men want ambition. *You* want ambition. This sounds like devil's advice, but I give it !'

He told me that undergraduates fresh from public schools often write better essays than when they have passed a term or two at Oxford. I am reminded of this when golf-players say that a person playing at golf for the first time often succeeds better than in his (or her) second attempt. Is it whimsical to suggest that, in the two instances, the explanation may be the same ? In the one case, as in the other, a novice who has just ceased to be a beginner is, as it were, dazzled by the increasing light. He seeks prematurely to attain hard and complicated results : *copia inopem facit.*

My father, who thoroughly disliked Froude's championship of Henry VIII., complained especially that the historian sets so much value on the preambles of Acts of Parliament ; and he added that the most iniquitous Act of Parliament is sure to have a plausible preamble. I asked Jowett whether he, too, did not think that the stress laid by Froude on those preambles is unwarrantable. ' It's a craze,' was the characteristic answer.

On my praising Shelley to Jowett at Byron's expense, he answered : ' I think that Byron was altogether a finer man than Shelley.'

I drew his attention to a passage in which Voltaire foreshadowed the principle of free trade. He observed, in reply, that a similar anticipation is to be found in Plato's ' Laws ' : in the ideal State no duty was to be levied either on exports or on imports. Plato, however, was, I think, for imposing restrictions on the exportation of arms.

In the hope of improving my Latin style, I at one time studied Muretus ; and I asked Jowett what he thought of him ' The best thing in him,' he replied, ' is where he praises the massacre of St. Bartholomew—' O præclarum illum diem !' Of course, he was not quite serious in what he then said, any more than in what he implied when, on my asking him long ago whether he wished to give the franchise to women, he merely answered, with a radiant smile : 'I have a friend who says that he would rather see England governed by her five most incapable men than by her five ablest women.' The view indicated in this last utterance of Jowett— a view which he seems to have modified in later life — may be well illustrated by a remark of Amiel :

Peut-être n'est-il pas bon qu'une femme ait l'esprit libre ; elle en abuserait tout de suite. Elle n'entre pas en philosophie sans perdre son don spécial qui est le culte de l'individuel, la défense des usages, des mœurs, des croyances, des traditions. Son rôle est de ralentir la combustion de la pensée. Il est analogue à celui de l'azote dans l'air vital. . . . Capable de tous les dévouements et de toutes les trahisons, 'monstre incompréhensible' à la seconde puissance, la femme fait les délices de l'homme et son effroi. .

Jowett once said in his odd way : 'I thought once of giving myself up to political economy, but I happened to become Professor of Greek.' But, though he spoke thus jestingly, he of course took the professorial duties most seriously. It may be instructive to contrast the way in which he regarded those duties with the way in which they were sometimes regarded in the last century. The delicious suggestion which was made by Lord Chesterfield to his son, then a lad in his sixteenth year, may illustrate this· 'What do you think of being Greek professor at one of our universities? It is a very pretty sinecure, and requires very little knowledge (much less than, I hope, you have already) of that language.'

He is well known to have been an economist of the old school, and an unwavering disciple of Ricardo. How thoroughly this was the case may be shown by some remarks addressed by him to a friend, who has reported the conversation to me, and who is himself at once a man of business and a man of letters. My friend told Jowett that, during the American Civil War, 100 dollars in gold sometimes equalled 240 in greenbacks, and sometimes 280. Once, on the occasion of a Northern victory, the change was from 280 to 255 in one day. 'I think you must be mistaken,' said Jowett; 'this doesn't square with Ricardo.' The friend explained that Ricardo's principles would be strictly applicable to practice if man were a mere automaton, unaffected by sudden impulses of hope or fear. Jowett at first seemed a little provoked, but at last exclaimed with his beaming smile, 'I am certainly right in theory, but perhaps you are right as to the facts.' And then he added, 'But read Ricardo.'

The same friend tells me that, on his speaking to Jowett of Rousseau as a great intellectual force, a momentary flash of asperity shot forth from his placid eye, and he exclaimed, 'No; he was a mere sentimentalist!' It was certainly strange that the Master was not attracted to Rousseau by the charm of his diction; for in general he had a keen sense for style. He once read to me Bacon's famous sentence, *Men fear death, as children fear to go in*

the dark; and then he added, 'Men can't write like
that now.'

Two pieces of advice given me by Jowett, with a
view to the formation of my style, may be worth
recording.   First, he wished me to take great pains
about the right use of connecting particles; and,
in general, to be careful about the orderly and
'logical' arrangement, and, as it were, dovetailing
of sentences.   Secondly, he told me to try to write
with 'feeling.'   This latter advice he himself put
into practice.   Indeed, the practice of it came
naturally to him.   It is sometimes possible to pick
holes in the construction of his sentences, but in
feeling his style is seldom or never deficient.   Let
me add that the word 'feeling' seems to denote the
quality which especially marks the passages of
poetry which he used to quote—the quality, moreover, which, when he quoted them, he brought out
by the peculiar music of his voice.   I seem at this
moment to hear that very peculiar music just as I
heard it more than thirty years ago, when he repeated to me the grim consolation which Achilles
offered to a son of Priam, whom he had known and
liked in days gone by, and for whom he seems to
have still retained as much affection as was com-
patible with his determination to kill him:

’Αλλὰ, φίλος, θάνε καὶ σύ τίη ὀλοφύρεαι οὕτως ;
Κάτθανε καὶ Πάτροκλος, ὅπερ σέο πολλὸν ἀμείνων.*

---

* 'Die, my friend though thou art; why dost thou vainly
lament?   Patroclus also died, who was a far better man than
thou.'

He warned me against mistaking what he called 'feeling' for the frequent use of metaphor. Indeed, he cautioned his pupils against over-indulgence in metaphor. To a pupil, who had been reading him an essay, he remarked : ' Your style is too flowery. The Chinese like a flowery style, we don't ; but,' he added, ' it is not a bad fault.'

' You are accustomed,' he said to me (in effect) after I had taken my degree, ' to write college essays. You will, of course, have to alter your style if you begin writing for the *Saturday Review*. One thing especially should be noted. You must, above all things, try to be clear when you are writing for the general reader. *Don't be too subtle for him.*' It is remarkable that he spoke so patiently of the possibility of my becoming a journalist ; for he seems to have felt a somewhat unaccountable horror of journalism, and particularly of writing for the daily papers. I am told that G. H. Lewes once extolled the daily press in his presence, and dilated in glowing terms on the mighty and beneficent weapon which is wielded by journalists. Jowett listened with an attention which at first seemed like acquiescence, but he presently rejoined : ' Why, yes ; *but, for my part, I'd rather break stones on the road !*' He is reported to have made use of this extravagant comparison in the same connection more than once.

Some of Jowett's literary and other judgments may be gathered from the following conversation with a friend, which occurred towards the close of the Master's life :

Friend.—Have you read Mrs. Grote's " Life of Grote "?'

J.—' Yes [laughing]—a curious book. It is really a history of Mr. and Mrs. Grote. . . . Mr. Grote was a great Radical in his youth; she told me that at first he did not like her asking her great relations to Threadneedle Street, but afterwards he said that rich men were very like others, except that they did not want to get anything out of you. Later he began to go out more, and once, when he asked a peer to dinner, she said: " Oh, George, who runs after the Lords now?" Does she speak of her friendship with Sydney Smith in the book ?'

F.—' I think not. Did you know him ?'

J.—' I never spoke to him; he was a Fellow of New College.'

F.—' Did you ever hear him preach ?'

J.—' Yes, once, in St. Paul's; I don't remember what he preached about.'

F.—' Was it amusing ?'

J.—' I think it was; he is the wittiest Englishman that ever lived, except Swift.'

*   *   *   *   *

F.—' Did you ever meet Mill at Mrs. Grote's house ?'

J.—' No; he died soon after I knew Mrs. Grote.'

*   *   *   *   *

F.—' I suppose you never read any modern novels now ?'

J.—' Yes, I do. I've read a good many this summer. I've read "David Grieve." .

F.—' I'm sure you did not like it.'

J.—' Yes, I did. I think it is a very good book.'

F.—' What else did you read ?'

J.—' I read " Tess "—a very powerful book—and " Esther Van Homrigh." I think it's a mistake to write historical novels. But Mrs. Woods has collected a great deal about Swift; she's done it very well. . . . The longer a man puts off his profession the better; but he musn't put off after his memory has reached its strongest—after thirty, I should say.'

*   *   *   *   *

F.—'Have you any objection to women speaking on plat-forms?'

J.—'Not if they do it well. —— and —— [two noted female orators] do a great deal of good. . . . The law is a good study. Every man who deserves to can succeed at the Bar. I say what Mr. Senior said, viz., four things are necessary: (i.) ability; (ii.) industry; (iii.) knowledge of the world; (iv.) health. Every man who has them will get on at the Bar. Literature plays such a great part in society and daily life that a man must have some knowledge of it.'

F.—'You don't think a knowledge of science can take its place?'

J.—'No.'

The distrust of historical novelists which Jowett indicated was probably connected with the fact that they are apt, as it were, to dip the past in the present, and that the result of such inopportune dipping must needs be something of a daub. An extreme example of this confusion is furnished by Ebers, who represents the Egyptian doctors, in the time of Moses, as exercising their minds over the morality of vivisection. I shall have occasion to recur to this mode of playing tricks with history further on. At present I will illustrate my meaning by saying that I called Jowett's attention to Walter Scott's statement, in 'Kenilworth,' that Varney lulled himself through Atheism into complete moral in-sensibility. Scott seems to imply that the use of this moral narcotic was not uncommon in those days. On the other hand, it seemed to me that, in Elizabethan times, Atheism must, to say the least, have been extremely rare; and that, even in our own day, villains nearly always find it easier to disregard religious sanctions than to disbelieve in them. Jowett in the main agreed with me ; but he thought that to the general rule there have been exceptions. One such exception he believed to have been Philippe le Bel.

Of Scott's novels his favourite was 'The Bride of Lammermoor.' This preference was shared by Matthew Arnold, who says that Falkland 'has for the imagination the indefinable, the irresistible charm of one who is and must be, in spite of the choicest gifts and graces, unfortunate—of a man in the grasp of fatality. Like the Master of Ravenswood, that most interesting by far of all Scott's heroes, he is surely and visibly touched by the finger of doom.' Jowett would, in the main, have sympathized with this striking passage, though he would doubtless have felt that Falkland's death at Newbury was a mere accident, and that it can therefore give no colour to the belief that men of his temperament are generally fated to die young.

It is sometimes said that Jowett, though Professor of Greek, was an indifferent scholar. Two facts bearing on this question may be worth mentioning. In my Oxford days I met a great Cambridge scholar who, shortly afterwards, was made a Bishop. On hearing that I was a pupil of Jowett, he talked to me about him, and declared, half in jest, that at Cambridge they could more easily forgive his heresy than his bad scholarship. When next I saw Jowett, I told him of my meeting with the distinguished Cantab, and asked his opinion of his scholarship.

'It seems presumptuous in me,' replied Jowett (in effect), 'to criticise his scholarship. But he does not seem to me to understand St. Paul. St. Paul's style is so peculiar that the ordinary rule of scholarship seemed to me to be not quite applicable to him.' According to this view, the Apostle's words are to be interpreted by reference to his modes of thought, and not merely his modes of thought by reference to his words. I speak subject to correction, but I think that Jowett, in the words just quoted, laid his finger on a line of demarcation which divides Oxford scholars as a class from Cambridge scholars as a class. My impression that this is so is confirmed by a letter which I have just received from a Cambridge scholar who is even more distinguished than the one already referred to, and who writes to me of Jowett: 'I always was grieved by the indefiniteness of his scholarship. He seemed to think that words and phrases had no particular meaning, while I was taught, and with all my heart believe, that "there is a mystery in every syllable" of St. Paul (say) or St. John.'

The other fact bearing on the question is this: That admirable scholar, Professor Conington, once said that Arthur Stanley came to him in sore discomfiture at the severity with which the critics had handled his edition of the Epistles to the Corinthians. With the frankness due from one old Rugbeian to another, he told Stanley that in some cases he had not a leg to stand upon, and must not think of replying to his critics. Of Jowett's scholarship Coning-

took a more favourable view. Personally, he might differ from some of Jowett's translations; but he thought that in every instance Jowett could make out a good case for himself.

A lady asked why it is that boys are so much slower in learning Latin and Greek than girls are in learning French and German; is it because Latin and Greek cannot be picked up in conversation? Jowett replied that the chief cause of the anomaly seems to be that the classical languages are so 'difficult'—difficult, that is, by reason of their unlikeness to English. One odd classical judgment of his may be worth mentioning. He did not care much for Demosthenes, though he admitted that Demosthenes had more of the *ars celare artem* than Thucydides had. But he seemingly thought that the great orator did not possess this art of concealment in its completest form. The art with which he concealed his art was not so perfect as to conceal itself. At any rate, Jowett preferred the rugged simplicity of the speeches reported or composed by Thucydides.

Shortly after I went up to Oxford, Jowett spoke to me slightingly of the usefulness of memory. He quoted Rochefoucauld's saying: 'Tout le monde se plaint de sa mémoire, personne ne se plaint de son jugement;' and he went on to say that nearly everyone has a memory good enough for the ordinary purposes of life, while in judgment nearly everyone is deficient. Afterwards he seemed to modify this view. I asked him whether Arthur Stanley's versatile and, as it were, ubiquitous memory was not unrivalled 'No,' he replied; 'Conington has a better memory than Stanley, but Stanley has a more useful memory.' He said that the memory of the man who could repeat a book of 'Paradise Lost,' after once reading it over, was simply a disease; but he thought that a memory powerful within reasonable limits—such a memory as Macaulay's—was of great value. A lady once asked him whether he thought that a good memory can be acquired. Pointing to a former pupil, who had and still has an abnormally retentive memory, he answered: 'A good memory may be often acquired, but not such a memory as *he* has.' It may be worth adding that a memory which is thus slow in losing, is sometimes also slow in acquiring. For example, the former pupil indicated by Jowett has no whist-memory. By taking pains, he could contrive to remember the trump-card of the first deal and his own cards, and he would remember them for a long time. But these fourteen cards would in a manner crowd out the cards of the subsequent deals, and, long before they had worked their way into his memory, his friends would be impatient for him to play.

In a trifling matter Jowett once showed a want of moral courage most unusual with him. When I was young I shared Kingsley's liking for a bracing air; and I perturbed my friends by telling them that I should beseech Jupiter to let east winds blow unceasingly over the Elysian fields! On my saying something of the sort to Jowett, he replied, with a

laugh : 'I also like east winds; but I am afraid to
confess it, for no one would believe me.' Having
thus trespassed into the hygienic province, I am
tempted to do so again. When I stayed with Jowett
at Freshwater, one of the party, recovering from an
illness, had the appetite of a convalescent. 'You
eat more,' said Jowett, 'than anyone I ever knew,
except a young lady who was told that if she didn't
eat eight mutton-chops a day she would die. So
she was brave, ate the eight mutton-chops, and
lived!' Many years later, when Jowett himself was
ailing and depressed, the friend to whom he made
this remark tried to cheer him by expressing a hope
that he would live to emulate the green and sprightly
old age of Dr. Lee, the Master of Balliol, about
whom Mrs. Thrale wrote to Dr. Johnson : 'Are you
not delighted with his gaiety of manners and youthful
vivacity now that he is eighty-six years old ? I never
heard a more excellent or perfect pun than his, when
someone told him how, in a late dispute among the
Privy Councillors, the Lord Chancellor struck the
table with such violence that he split it. "No, no,
no," replied the Master dryly; "I can hardly persuade myself that he split the table, though I
believe *he divided the board !*"'

On the occasion of my visit to Jowett at Freshwater, I heard him pass judgment on Browning.
He came across a statement in the *Saturday Review*
that we had one poet of the first order, but that we
had scarcely another who could be ranked even in
the second class. He stopped, looked straight before

him for a second, and then said: 'I think that Browning deserves a *shady first.*' To another friend Jowett admitted Browning's power, but said that he thought his style needlessly cumbrous and distorted. In truth, the relation between the two men seems to have been peculiar. Browning expressed great affection for Jowett, but complained that Jowett would never let him hear him preach. When he was staying with Jowett one Sunday, Jowett slipped away after breakfast and preached to the college servants, but gave Browning no hint. Browning said: 'He will let me talk to him and dine with him, but he will not let me pray with him.'

Another incident which occurred during my stay at Freshwater may be worth mentioning. Jowett took me to dine with the famous amateur photographer, Mrs. Cameron. He was in a taciturn mood; and it fell to my lot to do my full share of the talking and to draw out our hostess. As Jowett and I were walking home, he suddenly exclaimed: 'You asked too many questions.' As I was of full age, and thought myself capable of discerning between 'a time to keep silence and a time to speak,' I inquired: '*Did* I ask too many questions?' 'Far too many,' was the laconic answer. I forbore to press the matter further; but his censure wrought in me a mood similar to that which prompted Benjamin Franklin to say: 'As we must account for every idle word, so we must for every idle silence.'

It is well known that, in his old age, Jowett came

round to something like Franklin's opinion—came, in fact, to think that if silence is silver, good discourse is golden. He exhorted some of his pupils to keep commonplace books, and especially to jot down in them the best anecdotes that they heard; and he is said to have himself put these rules into practice. He had a yet quainter method of showing how completely he had faced round. With the zeal of a proselyte, this late convert from silence to sociability wrote a sermon on the art of conversation. The sermon was preached in Westminster Abbey and, less appropriately, in the wilds of Scotland. More strangely still, he took for his text: 'Man shall not live by bread alone, but by every word that proceedeth out of the mouth.' Ear-witnesses tell me that he sometimes gave the text in this form, and sometimes added the concluding words, 'of God.' In all cases, however, those words, so full of significance in the original text, were practically dropped out of the sermon. In fact, the 'ingenious Frenchman' who, according to Fitzjames Stephen, described that text as *cette belle et touchante parole de Chateaubriand*, can scarcely have done greater violence to its true meaning and manifold associations unconsciously than Jowett did consciously and deliberately.

A French writer has said that, 'On ne fait bien que ce qu'on fait habituellement.' It was not to be expected that Jowett would ever excel in conversation as some men excel in it who have made it the business of their lives. But undoubtedly he infused into it an ingredient which the most highly trained of mere talkers has not at his command; he seasoned it with his potent and penetrating personality. Hence arose the influence and the fascination which he exercised over the best women. Of the incidents that are reported in reference to his friendships with good women, only one need be here mentioned. The sister of an undergraduate who was ill at Balliol went to stay with the Master, and received from him the utmost kindness and attention. When she was taking leave, she first hesitated, and then said that before parting she would venture to ask a very particular favour. As she again hesitated, the Master grew uneasy and looked interrogative. At last, out came the request: 'Will you marry me?' He paced up and down, and blushed deeply as he replied: 'That would not be good either for you or for me.' It was now the young lady's turn to blush. 'Oh—oh—I meant to say I am going to be married, and would you perform the service?' Poor girl! she had been refused by Jowett without having proposed to him!

To some of my readers the foregoing anecdote may be familiar, but I repeat it, not merely because I find that it is less widely known than I imagined it to be or than it deserves to be, but also because it is in its main outlines authentic, and I wish to rescue it from the rising flood of scepticism which threatens to submerge all the good stories about Jowett. Nearly all the Jowett-tradition, so dear to undergraduates and gossips, is discovered to be little

better than a Jowett-legend, and, in Sir Thomas
More's phrase, 'many well counterfeit jewels make
the true mistrusted.' 'Well counterfeit' some
apocryphal stories about Jowett certainly are: so
much so that, if judged of merely by internal
evidence, the best of them would be pronounced
genuine. For instance: there is an old anecdote
that an examiner put the question, 'Why did the
Athenians condemn Socrates?' Some such answer
was given as that he was believed to be corrupting
the youth and undermining the national religion.
'No. He was put to death *for being a bore.*' The
terse irony of this saying has a Jowettian flavour
about it, but Jowett himself told me of the saying,
and it was to a Cambridge don that he ascribed it.

In 1891, after an absence of twenty years, I
revisited Oxford. It was hard for me to realize that
many of the undergraduates whom I saw around me
had not been born when I was last in the place, and
that none of them had been born when I took my
degree thirty-one years before. I learnt by degrees
how completely I was looking at the University
system from the outside, and, at last, it was only by
a strong effort that I could feel myself to be in any
sense an Oxford man. And thus it was with a
mingled pride and sadness that I found myself
exclaiming: 'Stantes erant pedes nostri in atriis
tuis, Oxonia.'*

Such reflections as these were brought home to

* Ps. cxxii. 2 (adapted). The Vulgate, I believe correctly,
here employs the past tense instead of the future (*stood* instead
of *shall stand*).

me by renewing my intercourse with Jowett. I took some notes of a conversation which I had with him that year, but those notes have been mislaid, and I must therefore confine myself to giving one or two points from memory. It was in that conversation that, as I mention further on, he surprised me by remembering some particulars of the visit that I had paid him twenty years before.

We talked about Mr. Francis Newman's recently published work concerning John Henry Newman —a work so well intended, and yet (as it were) so fratricidal, that, if Lady Byron could be called *the moral Clytemnestra of her lord*, Mr. Francis Newman might, at least, as justly be entitled the moral Timoleon of his brother. Jowett seemed to me not wholly to disagree with the view taken by Mr. F. Newman.

The two brothers appeared to Jowett to present a striking contrast. He regarded Mr. F. Newman as almost 'pedantic' in his strictness about literal truth. On the other hand, he described the Cardinal as comparatively 'indifferent to truth and morality' in the province of religion. At first this accusation startled me; but presently he so manipulated it that it lost much of its sting. The accusation, as I understood it, amounted merely to this: When he represented Newman as more or less indifferent to truth in theology, he merely meant that the Cardinal did not apply to the sacred history and literature of Palestine, and to the history and literature of the Church, the same canons of criticism which he would have applied to any other history or literature. But what shall we say of the charge of indifference to morality in religious matters? An extreme instance will best show what that charge really meant. To the respectable burghers of Jericho it would have seemed incredible that their disesteemed countrywoman, who, besides corrupting their private morals, gave treacherous aid to the public enemy, should have been singled out among all the inhabitants as the recipient of Divine favour. To Jowett, too, it was evidently incredible that so anomalous a selection could have been made. And what he complained of in Newman was that considerations of this sort, considerations involving a charge of injustice against God, produced less effect on him: not, indeed, than they have produced on the vast majority of Christians in all ages, but than they ought to have produced on a man of his ability in the nineteenth century.

On the whole, I gathered that Jowett had little sympathy with the Cardinal. Let me add that my general impression is confirmed by a friend who has told me that he heard Jowett complain of the large space which, in the 'Apologia,' is taken up with the motives which induced Newman to quit the Church of England for that of Rome; and that Jowett characteristically added: 'Not, I should have thought, a very important question.'

I expressed regret that Catholicism seemed unable, at present, at any rate, to shake off the belief in eternal punishment. Jowett replied that the

Catholics have a safety-valve in their doctrine of Purgatory.* I reminded him that, according to their belief, Hell lies below Purgatory, and that the poor wretches who are consigned to this nether region will not be suffered to rise *viâ* Purgatory to Heaven.† Enlightened Catholics, he rejoined, would reserve Hell 'for a few very wicked people'; all persons whom they or we care about would be started on the upward track. I asked whether he did not think that all Anglicans and other Protestants would shortly rid themselves of that spiritual anachronism, that interesting but repulsive survival of devil-worship. 'Voltaire,' he answered, 'declared that anyone who openly spoke or wrote against morality would be pelted. And one might almost say the same of any clergyman who should now preach in favour of eternal punishment.'

The reference to Voltaire tempts me, by way of digression, to mention that a friend tells me that he heard Jowett say that civilization owes more to

* Jowett seemed to me to be not wholly destitute of sympathy with Catholicism. I once expressed to him strong indignation at the Catholic practice of withholding the Bible from the people. Jowett replied that he regarded that practice as a mistake, but not as an unmixed evil; he added: ' It prevents the people from perplexing their minds with the Colenso difficulties.'

† A Catholic priest, after reading the passage in the text, writes to me : ' Did I ever tell you of a saying of Cardinal Manning on the hell question? A friend suggesting that it was a place of eternal suffering eternally untenanted, he answered: " If one did not hope that it was so, who could endure life ?" ' If ever Professor Mivart should relapse into his amiable heresy, let us hope that the spirit of the defunct Cardinal will be present among his judges !

Voltaire than to all the Fathers of the Church put together.

In my orthodox days I was struck by the glaring contrast between the asceticism of the early Christians and the luxurious living of our upper classes ; and, in my intercourse with Jowett, I gave expression to the compunctions which the contrast aroused in me. Regarding me as habitually over-scrupulous, he replied : ' The life of the early Christians was not very like your life at Peckforton, but it was not therefore better.'

On my once reminding him of the zeal with which Voltaire took up the cause of such victims of injustice as Lally Tollendal and Admiral Byng, he observed with a smile : ' That quite makes up for his being an infidel.'   I remember telling him that I had been assured that Miss Martineau, who was then living, not merely disbelieved in immortality, but gloried in the disbelief. ' It seems to me,' he said, ' very strange and unnatural, but she may be a good woman for all that.'

In 1892 and 1893 I again called on Jowett. My notes of what passed between us on these two latter occasions have been preserved, and I now publish them, premising that, as I am naturally anxious to ascribe nothing to him which he did not say, I have probably omitted much that he did say, and the result has been that I have not assigned to him his due share in the conversations.

May 30, 1892.—In reference to one of the most distinguished of living men, the remark was made that he could see only one side of a question, and that this limitation implies much self-deception. Adverting to the danger of self-deception, I quoted from Bacon's 'Essay on Truth': ' 'Tis not the lie that passeth through the mind, but the lie that sinketh in and settleth in it, that doth the hurt.' Jowett replied that he would rather make a friend of a man who practised self-deception than of one who consciously deceived others. I spoke of different forms of deception. Jowett objected to deception for a man's own interest. I replied that it was hard to define what would be directly or indirectly for a man's own interest. He explained that he did not mean 'for a man's highest interest.' I spoke of self-deception as being especially a feminine quality, and illustrated my meaning by a jocular example. If a man looked at a negro (or morally black man) who wished to be thought white, he, knowing all the time that he was speaking falsely, might tell him that he was not so very black. A woman would scruple to do this, but, after putting on a white veil, would first persuade herself, and then tell the negro, that he was not black at all. Jowett doubted whether there was much difference between an average man and an average woman in this respect.

Tollemache.—' Many of my best friends are women; but I am bound to add that women seem to me less accurate than men, and they are said to be less trustworthy witnesses in a court of justice.' He seemed doubtful whether this is so.

At this moment the Vice-Master came in, and

asked Jowett to propose a subject for the weekly essays. The Master suggested 'Authority in Matters of Science and Opinion,' and said to me: 'I think it good that the undergraduate should get clear ideas on this question.'

T.—'Will one essay do this for them?'

J.—'At any rate it will set them thinking about it. Didn't you write on this?'

T.—'*Indeed* I did. It reminds me of old times.' He said, with his Platonic irony: 'You have risen a great deal above this; but I am still trudging on in the old path.'

When the Vice-Master had left the room, a new subject was opened.

T.—'Why is it that many happy men are pessimists? Men often declare that they would not live their lives over again, and yet almost any man of thirty would prefer living another thirty years to being extinguished at once.'

J.—'Would he not find it rather monotonous?'

T.—'I assume the second period of thirty years to be equally happy with the first period, but not to be identical with it. If you put the case of a man living his life exactly óver again, you must suppose him to be dipped in Lethe before he runs the course a second time. Is it not because most people do not realize this that so many declare that they would at once refuse such an offer? A day which has one moment of acute pain, but is in all other respects to one's liking, would, if unforeseen, be justly counted a happy day. But if such a day were foreseen, the prospect of the moment of acute pain would cast its shadow over the fair prospect of the rest of the day. In like manner, if a man tries to conceive what it would be to live his life over again, his imagination insensibly turns to the painful or blameworthy episodes in that life.' Jowett showed some impatience at this mode of reasoning; indeed, he generally set his face against discussions not bearing on practice.

Wishing, however, to draw from him his real opinion on the saddening and deadening philosophy of Schopenhauer, I went on to defend optimism by giving such examples as the following: If life is not worth living, ought not the present inhabitants of Smyrna to set up a statue to Tamerlane, in recollection of the wholesale and somewhat picturesque beneficence wherewith he relieved eighty thousand of their predecessors of the burden of existence, and made a pyramid of their skulls? Nay, further, we are justly incensed at the brutal Roman who caused his infirm slaves to be eaten by his lampreys. But the mode of death to which these poor wretches were subjected was probably not more painful than that which Nature would otherwise have had in store for them. All, therefore, that the tyrant did for them was to shorten their span of life. So that, when we execrate him and pity his victims, we virtually imply that even the decrepit old age of a Roman slave contained a *plus* quantity of happiness —that it was a boon rather than the reverse. Hence I concluded that, 'unless a man is meditating suicide, he implies in every act of his life that he thinks his life worth living.'

J. (with deliberation and earnestness).—'Why yes, yes, we imply this *always*. In brief, we may say that a disciple of Schopenhauer is a sort of *should-be* suicide, or, rather, that the whole question *solvitur vivendo*.'

He urged me to go on writing, and advised me to write on 'Popular Fallacies.' I asked him whether he meant something in the style of Charles Lamb.

J.—'No, I mean something more serious than that.* Something in the style of Sydney Smith's paper on "The Fallacies of Bentham."' The mention of Sydney Smith suggested a question on the difference between wit and humour. I quoted the view of a living writer, that wit consists in seeing analogies, and humour in seeing contrasts.

J.—'I do not think this will hold. The difference seems to be that wit consists in a number of points, while humour is continuous.'

T.—'Might not your view of wit and humour be otherwise expressed by saying that wit is humour crystallized, and humour is wit in solution?'

J.—'Possibly.'

T.—'Would you not say that Sydney Smith has wit, and not humour?'

J.—'He has both.'

A phrase which Sydney Smith himself used

* Jowett once intimated to me, and he seems to have said plainly to at least one other pupil, that he had no great admiration for the writings of Lamb.

virtually ascribed to Maria Edgeworth humour in Jowett's sense of that word: 'She does not say witty things, but there is such a perfume of wit runs through all her conversation as makes it very brilliant.'

In consideration of my bad eyesight, he accompanied me downstairs. In doing so he leant on my arm, and quoted the couplet from the 'Anthology':·

Ἀνέρα τις λιπόγυιον ὑπὲρ νώτοιο λιπαυγὴς
Ἦγε πόδας χρήσας ὄμματα χρησάμενος.*

'No,' he added, with a smile, 'we are not quite the lame man riding on the blind man, for you can see a little and I can walk a little.'

May 7, 1893.—Jowett said that England seemed to him to run great risk of an invasion in the next fifty years; he thought there might be peril from Russia.

T.—'Is not Russia weakened by Nihilism?'

J.—'Not so much by Nihilism as by corruption. But even so, the mass would obey the Czar. He will in a few years be able to put five million in the field.'

T.—'That is like Xerxes.'

J.—'Yes, but they will be very different men from the Persians.'

T.—'Shall not we be supported by Germany, Austria, and Italy?' He seemed doubtful about

---

* Once did a strong blind man set a man that was lame on his shoulders;
Feet to the cripple he lent, borrowing eyes in return.

Austria and Italy. He spoke of China as another source of danger to Western civilization, adding that, with its vast numbers and indifference to life, it has the making of a great military power.

We spoke of the recently-published ' Life of Lord Sherbrooke' (Lowe), to which both he and I had contributed reminiscences.

J.—'Lowe was in reality a thorough Liberal to the last.'

T.—' Not, surely, a democratic Liberal!'

J.—'No, but a philosophical Liberal. He had been on bad terms with the clergy, and was to the last anti-ecclesiastical.' He went on to intimate that Lowe was not wholly in the wrong; all history shows that religions become corrupt if they cease to keep terms with morality; if we are to tolerate the Church, she must be tolerant.

T.—'Have not Evolution and Biblical Criticism thrown the Church on the defensive, and made her more tolerant than she ever was before?'

J. — ' Look at the damnatory clauses in the Athanasian Creed. If the clergyman who repeats them regards them as a mere dead letter, his conduct is not favourable to a high morality. If he believes in them, he imputes to God a very low morality.'

T.—'I tell my American friends that when they discard the damnatory clauses they imply that the rest of the Creed is to be taken literally; and that thus, in the true sense of the saying, they make the *exception prove the rule.*'

J.—' I would give up the Creed altogether.'

T.—' Then would you not imply that the Apostles' and the Nicene Creeds are to be taken literally ?'

J.—' Every Church or Dissenting body must use compromise a little.'

T.—' People call the Broad Church clergy dishonest. But they praise Marcus Aurelius up to the skies. And yet did not he, the Pontifex Maximus, the Pope of paganism, practise conformity as completely as any Broad Church clergyman does now ?' Jowett assented, but pointed out that, on the other hand, some philosophers tried to spiritualize paganism ; and this he considered the nobler course. He quoted the example of Socrates. I remarked that Socrates poured a libation to the Sun, and vowed a cock to Æsculapius. Not only did he thus cause the death of the poor little cock, but he implied that Æsculapius took pleasure in its sacrifice. This was giving countenance to vulgar superstition.

J.—' Yes, I suppose this might be called an eccentricity. Perhaps he would not have much liked to be cross-questioned as to why he did it.' I hinted that he might have thought, as many Broad Churchmen now think, that a certain alloy of supernaturalism is the only way in which spiritual truths can be made to pass as current coin among the masses ; or (to vary the metaphor) spiritual food should be not raw, but cooked for the infirm digestions of the multitude.

J.—' I think that in the present day a religion without miracles would suit many people better than a religion with miracles.' I hinted that he was falling back on the theology of James Martineau, and that this stronghold is commonly thought to be not impregnable. It is open to attack from the disciples of Butler. If there is so much evil in the scheme of Nature, why not in that of Revelation? If in this life, why not in the next?

J.—' This seems to me to be taking the question entirely at the wrong end.' I wished to cross-question him, but I was not sure whether he was not thinking of himself when he said that Socrates would not have liked to be cross-questioned. I therefore restrained the impulse; and especially I avoided expressing surprise that a severe criticism on the practice of economy of truth should have proceeded from an ultra Broad Church clergyman— from one, that is, who in his official character had to be practising economy of truth continually.

I asked him how he explained the word ' but ' in the last line of the stanza wherein Tennyson expresses his trust ·

> ' That not a worm is cloven in vain;
> That not a moth with vain desire
> Is shrivelled in a fruitless fire,
> Or *but* subserves another's gain.'

He regarded ' or but subserves ' as equivalent to ' without subserving.' I, on the other hand, insisted that the word ' but ' must mean ' only,' and that the whole passage implies a hope that there will be a heaven even for the moths and worms.

J.—' Would not that be an extravagant view to

take ?' Extravagant it may be, but it is hardly unintelligible, especially in a poet. Whenever a poet or a sentimentalist argues from the Divine Love that all human suffering must be designed for the good of the sufferer, he is apt to be met with the objection : 'If this argument is worth anything, it must be applicable to the lower animals. Are you prepared to contend that all animal suffering makes for the good of the sufferer ?' To which objection the heart rather than the head is fain to make answer : ' Is such an aspiration wholly inadmissible ? Is it quite impossible that the involuntary suicide of a shrivelled moth may have been ordained for the ultimate good of that moth, which must mean for its posthumous good ?' It seems to me that some such vague hope as this may have been present to the poet's mind when he wrote the line in question.*

Jowett, as we have seen, thought otherwise. He however, seemed to modify his opinion, for he said

---

* I sometimes think that the lower animals bear the same sort of relation to Man that the Apocrypha bears to the Bible. Theologians are apt to regard the human soul and the Bible as having a right (so to speak), each in its own way, to say ' Noli me tangere ' to science. The lower animals and (though in a very different manner) the Apocrypha bar such exorbitant claims. They serve as intermediate links, and thus tend to *evolutionize* Religion. In other words, the lower animals are half human, just as the Apocrypha is half Biblical. The difficulty connected with the lower animals is noted in the text. As regards the Apocryphal writings, it is enough to remark that the very late Book of Enoch is quoted as authentic by St. Jude. In my youth I asked Jowett whether the Book of Enoch is not believed to have been discovered. ' There is no doubt whatever that it has been discovered,' he replied, with a certain heterodox zest.

that Tennyson probably wrote that under the influence of some of the writers of the last century.

T.—'Do you mean the Cambridge Platonists?'

J.—'No; I am chiefly thinking of Butler; but it will never do to apply such logic as yours to the words of the poet.'

As I rose to take my leave, he said: 'I believe that a great deal more is to be done to improve the condition of mankind, and that the great comfort for each of us is to feel that he has done, and is doing, something towards it.' Of course I assented, but I recalled Tennyson's counsel to beware lest

> 'In seeking to undo
> One riddle and to find the true
> I knit a hundred others new,'

and hinted that a somewhat similar warning should be addressed to enthusiastic reformers and world-betterers of all sorts.

J.—'Well, well, perhaps you're right. Good-bye.' These are the last words I heard him utter.

II.

'Equidem, ex omnibus rebus, quas mihi aut Fortuna aut Natura tribuit, nihil habeo quod cum amicitiâ Scipionis possum comparare.'—CICERO.

(Of all the benefits which Nature or Fortune has conferred on me, none can I compare with the friendship of Scipio.)

IN my Oxford days I was struck by a comment on Jowett which was made to me by one who had long been in close relations with him, and whose praise carries with it all the more weight because he himself was of the opposite party. After the lapse of more than thirty years, I feel confident that I can give the exact sense of what was said to me, though not in general the exact words; the few expressions that I can quote *verbatim* shall be printed in italics. 'There are two things in Jowett,' said my friend, '*besides the beautiful purity of his moral character,* which I especially admire: first, his power of seeing through and through a philosophical question, and, secondly, his power of stimulating men to work. *In these two qualities he is facile princeps of all men that I ever knew.* But I distrust his judgment of men. Some men, when writing for him their weekly essays, manage to bring into them some of his opinions expressed in his own peculiar way. These men he overrates; and, by comparison, he under-rates others. *His geese are sometimes swans, and his swans are sometimes great geese.'* This candid, and, at the same time, kindly, criticism may serve as a sort of text for the following remarks.

I will provide myself likewise with another help towards my attempted explanation of Jowett's character and opinions. A friend tells me that, when examined *vivâ voce* by Jowett, he sought to embellish one of his answers with some curious information. Jowett stared at him for a few moments, and then chirped : ' That's very true, but I don't see what it has to say to my question.' At the risk of incurring a like charge, the charge of irrelevance, I will seek to illustrate Jowett's modes of thought and feeling by comparing and contrasting the ground taken by him with the ground taken by Pattison—the standpoint of a modern Zwingli with the standpoint of a modern Erasmus.

The most obvious point of contrast between the two men is one which, being an admirer of Pattison, I approach with uneasiness, and, indeed, by a circuitous path. Mr. Mill, in 1864, told me that he did not know Jowett personally, but added with emphasis that he felt the greatest admiration for him. He went on to say that he had come to take a hopeful view of the method of teaching which then prevailed at Oxford; but that he had regarded the method which formerly prevailed there with strong dislike ; nay, I think he said, with ' abhorrence.' In saying this, he seemed to me to be implying that the improvement was in great measure due to Jowett, partly, that is, to his direct action, and partly to his example. It must be candidly admitted that this praise could not have been bestowed on Pattison, who, his enemies declared, threw his Rectorial duties to the winds. I once spoke on this unpleasant subject to Matthew Arnold, who thereupon reminded me that in Pattison's youth public opinion expected far less from the Head of a college than it now does. I am only too glad to plead this apology for him, but I must take leave to remark that Pattison's excuse is Jowett's praise. The two men were contemporaries, and if the standard recognised in their youth was such that Pattison did not fall below it, what shall we say of Jowett, who rose so enormously above it ? In justice to Pattison, it should be added that this difference between his standard and Jowett's is connected with their conceptions of what a University should be. Jowett held that a University should be, above all things, a place of tuition. On the other hand, Pattison wished to model Oxford after the fashion of a German University—to make it a sort of nursery-garden, a *pépinière*, of research. Did not Pattison, both directly and indirectly, help on this ideal of research? What he achieved in that direction should count for much in his favour ; what he would have achieved, if his life had been prolonged, should count for more. If he had written a work

likely to endure, it would, at the not over-moral bar
of posterity, have atoned for his educational sins
not less fully and far more reasonably than 'Go,
lovely Rose,' has atoned for the sins of Waller.*
But this was not to be. He was to die, as he wrote
to a friend, 'leaving " Scaliger " unfinished.' Yet,
even as it is, even in spite of those educational sins
of his, and in spite also of literary incompleteness,
he stands forth conspicuous as the great Rector of
Lincoln—scarcely less conspicuous, indeed, than
Jowett stands forth the great Master of Balliol.

It need hardly be said that Jowett's supreme
success as a teacher was in great part due to the
strong personal interest which he felt in his pupils
and which he made them feel that he felt. That
interest extended even to their games. Of course he
would never have allowed the Balliol eleven to seek
delights and shun laborious days, nor, indeed, would
he have let cricket or any other game interfere with
the discipline of the college. Still, he was in a

* Macaulay, it is true, denies that Waller, by writing a few
flowing lines, has given a sufficient bribe to induce posterity to
condone the delinquencies of his public life. But, in truth,
has not the bribe been effectual ? Would not a Waller of the
present day prefer having the picture or autograph of Edmund
Waller to having the pictures or autographs of any number of
Wallers who lived and died in respectable insignificance ?
Nay, further; Burke, writing to a friend, remarked, with
evident satisfaction, that his residence at Beaconsfield ' was
formerly the seat of Waller the poet, whose house, or part of
it, makes at present the farmhouse within an hundred yards of
me.' There were probably not a dozen of Waller's contemporaries in regard to whom that most high-minded of politicians
would have felt a like satisfaction. Truly, the irony of fate,
or, as we may say, the irony of fame, is a queer thing.

certain sense a philathlete, which was all the more creditable to him because he was himself the very reverse of athletic. Once I walked with him near where some men were practising cricket, and a ball fell near his feet. He tried to throw it back to the bowler, but he threw it with very little force and considerably above an angle of forty-five degrees. I hope he did not hear the ill-repressed titter which arose from the ground, or the exclamation, ' Do look at Jowler shying!' to which some rude man gave utterance. Incidents of this sort make us wonder what Jowett can have been like as a young man. Our first impression is that he must have been a mere recluse. But this impression is erroneous. One who knew him as an undergraduate says that he was generally popular, and was a genial, if not jovial, companion.

It appears that he was in the quadrangle when he heard of his election to his Fellowship. He at once testified his joy by leaping as high as he could, and he was carried round the quadrangle on the shoulders of his friends. It is well known that, as Master, he subscribed a large sum (I think £3,000) to the purchase of the Balliol cricket ground, which, as he told me, he wished to save from the builder; and during his last summer, when he could take very little exercise, he would often go and look on at the cricket matches. In matters of this sort Pattison was the very antipodes of Jowett. If any student whom he thought worth anything devoted himself to games beyond what was absolutely necessary, he would probably have said that such devotion was, in fact, to misconceive or disregard the true end of recreation—was *propter ludum ludendi perdere causas*. At any rate, he would not have shared the sympathetic glow with which Jowett saw his pupils make the best of the spring-time of life; nor could he, if he would, have given the same hearty response to the wise man's exhortation, ' Rejoice, O young man, in thy youth.'

A letter which I have received from an able pupil of Jowett's contains some suggestive remarks bearing on this subject: ' I was always struck with his desire to bring (as Disraeli would have said) the peer and the peasant together. When he sent me his appeal for "Balliol Field," the new college cricket ground, the bringing of all classes of undergraduates together was one of the avowed motives. As a host he used to mingle his guests on this principle, and I do not think it proved successful. The social extremes, so marked under him at Balliol, led to its sets and cliques being strongly marked.'

But assuredly it was not only or chiefly by encouraging the college games that Jowett showed the deep interest which he felt in his pupils. His interest in them was manifold, and often took unexpected forms. Sometimes he surprised them by his memory of small particulars concerning them. A trifling instance of this came early under my notice. When I got the Balliol scholarship in 1856, the subject given us for Latin verses was a singular one: ' The Britannia Tubular Bridge.' On this spirit-stirring theme I wrote some rhapsodical non-sense about a Cambrian nymph bewailing the unsightly desecration of her solitude, and I was foolish enough to expect Jowett to admire what I had written, and I even fished for a compliment from him. He cut me short by exclaiming, with a provoking smile: 'You had one good line: "Atque suum ponti nomen posuere Britanni."' At the time I felt crestfallen, but afterwards I became crest-risen as I wondered how Jowett's well-stored memory had found room for this commonplace hexameter. Another and far more striking instance of Jowett's friendly memory, as I may call it, fell under my observation much later, when, in 1891, I revisited Oxford after an absence of twenty years. On seeing me, Jowett remarked how long it was since I had last paid him a visit, and then said: 'I think it is about twenty years,' and went on to mention some of those whom I had met at his house. A memory of this sort is occasionally found among men of leisure, though even among them it seems to be unusual; but that a busy man like Jowett should accomplish such a feat is as amazing as, to me certainly, it was flattering. The cultivation of this power of recalling minute details about friends was recommended by Lord Chesterfield to his son as an important factor in what he considered the art of arts—the art to please.

This personal memory, therefore, of Jowett was at once an effect and a symptom of the devoted interest which he took in his pupils, and may have helped to produce that unrivalled power of stimulating men to

work which was noted by his friendly critic. Can
that devoted interest have been connected with the
propensity to confound geese and swans which was
ascribed to him by the same critic? For myself,
I should have placed more reliance on Pattison's
judgment than on Jowett's in determining whether
this or that able youth was ever destined to do great
things. Pattison was a more dispassionate observer.
In reply to a question of mine about a man who had
not fulfilled the promise of his early days, he said,
not over kindly: 'He coached with me. He didn't
want my help, and I was ashamed to take his money.
I saw at once that he was a dead first. But he has
never made an original remark, or said anything worth
listening to.' And he gave me to understand that he
had foreseen his pupil's life-long sterility of ideas as
soon and as surely as he had foreseen his first class.
In fact, an able undergraduate was to Pattison a sort
of intellectual silkworm—a slow, narrow, unattractive
creature which must be tended for what may some
day be drawn from it. A silkworm fancier, let me
add, in forming an opinion as to what sort of silkworm will yield the best cocoon, is not likely to have
his judgment warped by personal predilection in
favour of any individual silkworm or class of silk-
worms. This may serve to illustrate the impartial
discernment of Pattison. In seeking to find a hidden
intellectual treasure he could wield the divining rod
more skilfully than Jowett. Also, he was more
concentrated on the quest. The professors at
Leipsic or Vienna owe some of their success in

casting the musical horoscope of their pupils to the
fact that they limit their attention to the best pupils,
and consider, in regard to each pupil, not whether
he will play well enough to give pleasure in a draw-
ing-room, but whether he has a chance of rising to
high rank as a professional. In like spirit, Pattison
desired that some of his pupils should become highly
distinguished. Jowett, on the other hand, was more
anxious that as many pupils as possible should stand
on the second or third plane of culture than that the
very few should stand on the first plane. *Comparatively* few, however, were the pupils who en-
grossed his interest, for, in truth, he was in his way
an intellectual aristocrat. As Sydney Smith succeeded in naturalizing the mongrel and ungracious
word *foolometer*, I hope I may express my meaning
by saying that Jowett was anything but a foolophilist.
I remember being somewhat shocked when Henry
Smith told me that Jowett, speaking of a very
amiable young man who at first showed small signs
of ability, observed: 'That man ought never to have
been let into the college.' In justice to the Master, and
also in confirmation of what was said of the untrust-
worthiness of his judgments upon men, I will
mention that he afterwards found that he had been
mistaken, and frankly acknowledged his error. Still,
the severity of his original remark shows wherein,
as an educator, he differed from Dr. Arnold. Dr.
Arnold was able to cast a spell over a large number
of morally earnest pupils who were willing to resign
themselves to his ascendancy, and who were what

Montaigne would have called *instruisables*, and what Sydney Smith would have called *philomaths*. Jowett, on the other hand, could exert an influence only through sympathy; and between him and unintellectual persons (at least of the male sex), sympathy, as a rule, there was none. I heard him say in one of his lectures that Plato sometimes seems to have been not far from the kingdom of heaven; but that Plato's heaven was not a spiritual, but an intellectual one. This remark of Jowett's might, in some degree, be taken as a parable applicable to himself. But I hasten to add that, though his influence could hardly ever be brought to bear except on a nature with which he was in sympathy, yet, when once called into activity, it penetrated and leavened the disciple's whole being, moral as well as intellectual.

I have insisted at length on the limitations of Jowett's direct influence, because those limitations serve to explain one special turn which that influence took. He is reproached with having unduly courted the society of the great. Is there any ground for this reproach? Well, let us at once acknowledge that he saw more of a few pupils who united great ability with high rank, than of many other pupils who had the ability without the rank. But those who urge this preference against him as a reproach would do well to add that, if he sought the company of the great men of this world, he did innumerable acts of kindness to the small men of this world; he helped needy students by gratuitous tuition as well as in more direct ways. It would seem, moreover, that the stress laid on this charge of tuft-hunting is indirectly a compliment to Jowett, for it shows that he is judged by an ideal standard. George Eliot, after referring to the single shortcoming of Rufus Lyon's life, remarks that a specially severe 'penalty will remain for those who sink from the ranks of the heroes into the crowd for whom the heroes fight and die.' In fact, no man who has once stood on the heroic pedestal can step down from it with impunity; to the sinning saint a double portion of blame is meted out. This may explain what has befallen Jowett. So bright and radiant is the surface which his whole character presents to view, that the smallest speck on it, nay, the merest shadow cast on it from without, at once attracts notice. The great men of this world are generally the best able to help one in time of need; they are also able to talk at first hand of truly great men and great actions; and in their company truly great and wise men will sometimes be met. So manifest is all this, that the courting of such profitable acquaintances is generally thought to be, at worst, venial. Of all the men who lived and died many centuries ago, there is perhaps none whom we regard with a feeling so akin to personal friendship as Horace. And yet he frankly proclaims that to have given pleasure to princes is no small credit to a man; and he adds that he himself, though poor and the son of a freedman, had found favour with generals and statesmen, and indeed that, upborne on mighty wings, he had risen high above the nest in which

he first saw the light.* We are none of us disposed
to judge Horace severely, because he was unflinch-
ingly loyal to his republican friends, and also because,
if he tuft-hunted, he carried on the embarrassing
chase, not through a dark and tortuous alley, but
along the highroad and in broad daylight. Still, he
pursued the quarry for its own sake; he had not,
and never pretended to have, any ulterior motive of
philanthropy. In this respect his case was wholly
unlike that of Jowett. If Jowett made friends with
men of station, he did so with a very distinct ulterior
object—with the object of doing them good, and
doing others good through them. We have seen
that he had no power to act directly on the masses;
but he thought it his duty to act on them somehow,
and therefore he acted on them indirectly. He made
it his aim to guide the leaders of the people and to
train their teachers — *custodire* ¦*custodes et docere
doctores.* With this view he brought his strong
personality to bear on men of intellectual eminence,
and especially on men who combined intellectual
with social eminence; for he held that social
eminence is an instrument wherewith, even at the
present day, the masses may be moved. The
decrepit and dying hand of the old aristocracy still
rests on the political lever; and he probably feared

---

* ' Principibus placuisse viris non ultima laus est.
  *   *   *   *   *
 Me libertino natum patre, et in tenui re
 Majores pennas nido extendisse loqueris.
  *   *   *   *   *
 Me primis urbis belli placuisse domique.'

that, as soon as that hand falls from it, then, instead of ceasing to act, the irrepressible lever will be manipulated by demagogues, and the last state of the community will be worse than the first. I say that he *probably* feared this, because, on the issue in question, which is practically the issue between modern Conservatism and modern Liberalism, he seems to have wavered in judgment; but, as will appear further on, in his later years he inclined to Conservatism. At present, it is enough to repeat that, if he ever did anything which even malice could misconstrue into tuft-hunting, he did it with a good object. He seems also to have done it with a good effect. One who ought to be well informed tells me that he believes that, when the private Memoirs of our time are brought to light, it will appear that Jowett, through his friends, compassed results in which he is now thought to have had no share; and, in particular, that he may thus have touched secret springs which carried his wishes to dispensers of patronage in high places, without, peradventure, those dispensers suspecting from what quarters the original impulse came. A Basque proverb reminds us that ' The needle, itself naked, clothes others.' It is possible that Jowett's career was a practical commentary on this. Can the irony of his situation have been such that he, to whom no Government gave, or, probably, dared to give, even a Canonry, may yet have been able with unseen hand to give a lift to the fortunes of others?

I have thus attempted to show that what is sometimes represented as a defect in Jowett's character may have arisen from his moral earnestness. Can he have drawn any intellectual defect from the same source? This question was to some extent answered when it was contended above that his opinion of his pupils and friends was warped by his ardent sympathy; and that, in respect of such judgments, Pattison, with his impartiality, born of comparative indifference, may have had an advantage over him. Other considerations point to the same conclusion. In my 'Recollections of Pattison,' I suggested that the Rector's moral apathy may have been partly due to his resolution to see things exactly as they are. One passage, illustrative of my argument, I will venture to quote:

' When a man labours to avert or to postpone a change which he regards as hurtful or premature, it is hardly possible for him to avoid exaggerating the evils of that change, and thus becoming an alarmist. When another or the same man seeks to evolve the energy needful for carrying out some great reform or establishing a scientific truth, it is perhaps impossible for him to avoid greatly exaggerating the importance of his under- aking, and thus becoming a strong optimist.'

The view here expressed marks the difference between the sage's and the saint's way of looking at things. The sage may be said to see the moral world represented in an ordinary map, in which the mountains and valleys are merely indicated. The saint, on the other hand, has before him a relief-map, in which the mountains and valleys—the ups and downs, that is, of human life and of human conduct —are represented so that they can be felt, and are represented also on a disproportionate scale. Voltaire, in one of his romances, tells how a gigantic native of Sirius chanced to stray on to our earth and with difficulty descried the puny race of men, whose tiny voices he managed to hear by means of an ear-trumpet, made of the paring of one of his own nails, and whose language he somehow understood. He deigned to interrogate one of those miserable beings, as he called them, whom God in His inscrutable wisdom had made so near to nothingness. In reply to his questions, one of the pigmies explained that it was for his own sake and that of his fellow-pigmies that the universe and all that therein is, including the people of Sirius, had been called into being. Whereupon the giant laughed so immoderately that the priggish little company who were assembled on his hand fell off and disappeared in the recesses of his clothes.* Has Voltaire, in concocting this tale, transgressed the bounds of legitimate caricature? Is it not the case that all saints, unconsciously or half unconsciously, conceive human weal to be the pivot round which all things turn? A hard blow was dealt to the old order of beliefs when our little planet was dislodged from the centre of the universe; and it is hardly too much to affirm that every saint, nay, every ardent moralist, is a would-be disciple of

* In a like spirit Renan has more than once compared mankind to an ants' nest. The following passage is characteristic: ' Soyons tranquilles : si nous sommes de ceux qui se trompent, qui travaillent à rebrousse-poil de la volonté suprême, cela n'a pas grande conséquence. L'humanité est une des innombrables fourmilières où se fait dans l'espace l'expérience de la raison ; si nous manquons notre partie, d'autres la gagneront.'

Ptolemy.* Now, not only was Jowett an ardent moralist : he was a devoted teacher of the young. And, like other teachers of the young, he had to keep his eye fixed on those small faults to which the young are specially liable, and which, if not rooted out, threaten to become serious. Persons who through long years dwell on those small faults are in danger of becoming living illustrations of the truth of that weighty and suggestive saying of Goethe, that the continuous use of the microscope interferes with the normal use of the eye. They are apt to become morally penny - wise, if not farthing-wise. Thus, to the Epicurean philosopher who regards the Stoical moralist as transforming molehills into real hills, the pedagogue must seem to exalt them into mountains of the Himalayan range. Jowett was far too much of a philosopher to be a pedagogue of this sort. But herein lay his weakness as well as his strength. He tried to be a philosopher, moralist, and preceptor all at once. As a philosopher, he looked at the world from the outside ; and, so looking, he dimly perceived—or (what is much the same thing) he was conscious of trying not to perceive—that all is vanity. As a moralist, he looked at the world from the inside, and almost convinced himself that all is an intense

* Some confirmation of this view is contained in the ingenious work which Dr. Whewell oddly entitled ' The Plurality of Worlds.' In seeking to batter down the belief in that plurality, the author was evidently, nay, avowedly, anxious to show that man is the head of the universe, and the climax of the creation of God.

reality. I hope it is not an over-strained meta-phor to add that, if he looked at the world with one eye, as it were, from the outside, and with the other eye from the inside, the result could hardly fail to be an occasional obliquity of mental vision.

After bringing this somewhat paradoxical charge against Jowett, the least I can do is to try to sub-stantiate it at once. The means of substantiating it would seem to be afforded by his unfriendly attitude towards Evolution. The future fame of Darwin, indeed, he foresaw at a time when the Newton of biology was thought ridiculous, or worse, by the religious world.* I had heard the concluding speech which Cockburn, as Attorney-General, made at the trial of William Palmer for poisoning. The speech so impressed me that, with youthful impetuosity, I thought that so great an orator could do anything; and I naïvely expressed regret to Jowett (in or about 1860) that Cockburn had not devoted himself to science; would he not, as a lawyer, leave behind him a posthumous reputation less enduring than Darwin's? 'A great deal less,' replied Jowett; 'but you cannot expect a man, in choosing his line of success in life, to think only of his reputation after death.' The remark was obvious enough; but I quote it partly because, seasoned as it was with his

* An example of this may be worth mentioning. A guest of my father's reminded me in his presence that I had promised to lend her the ' Origin of Species.' ' If I were Lady ——,' he said, ' I should first borrow it and then burn it. It seems to me so unscriptural.'

peculiar mode of utterance, it had a slight flavour of
the worldly wisdom which was sometimes discernible
in what he said to his pupils, and partly because it
showed that, when first the 'Origin of Species' appeared, he foresaw its great vogue. But his belief
in Evolution did not grow as the belief of others
in it grew. Perhaps the 'Descent of Man' gave
him a shock. Shortly after that volume appeared
I talked to him about Evolution. He at once admitted that he believed the origin of all species to
have been due to natural causes. But in regard to
Darwinism he added: 'I own that I feel rebellious.
How did the monkeys get rid of their hairs? It
would be absurd to suppose that they pulled them
out one by one.'* Whether, or how far, Jowett was
serious when he talked thus extravagantly, I no
more know than I know whether the Platonic
Socrates was serious when he talked no less extravagantly about the properties of the perfect
number, or whether Plato's conscience was at ease
when he ascribed to his revered master opinions
which, he well knew, were not his master's, but his
own. But, at all events, Jowett was serious when, in
1889, he wrote me the letter from which I give the

---

* Since writing the above, I have learnt that Jowett told
Dean Fremantle that he considered the 'Origin of Species' one
of the greatest and most far-reaching books that had appeared
in this century; but that, when the 'Descent of Man' came
out, he said: 'I don't believe a word of it,' without giving any
reason for the opinion thus confidently expressed. It sounds
as if he had taken for a motto: 'Sic volo, sic credo.' How
strange that such a man should have thought to oppose his
non possumus or *non volumus* to the plain evidence of science!

following strange extract. I omit the name of the distinguished evolutionist to whom he refers :

'I have read some part of ——'s writings, and do not think much of them. That which I read seemed to me only to say that the brain, as seen through the microscope, is infinitely complex; and the mind, of which we are conscious, is also infinite in complexity. This is not much to tell us. I think that physiologists, instead of boasting about Darwinism, which pretends so much and adds so little to our knowledge, have reason to feel rather humiliated at the faint light which they are able to throw on the relation of mind and body; nothing to explain the memory, which seems most allied to sense, nothing to assist in regulating the passions.'

In reply, I suggested to him that the evolutionist in question probably meant to point out how completely that complex thing the mind seems dependent on that complex thing the brain; if part of the brain is removed, the mind is liable to be impaired in a more or less ascertained way. Whence follows the obvious question : How is it possible that consciousness can survive the decomposition of the brain? But of this difficulty, which I was and am most anxious to see removed, he never at any time offered a solution.

Pattison, on the other hand, accepted Evolution, and mastered its principles as completely as an unscientific man can hope to master them. Probably he regarded Evolution as a convenient stone to throw at his orthodox antagonists and would-be persecutors. I had almost said that he would have liked to throw the stone at Stoical moralists. At any rate, I feel convinced that it was as a Stoical moralist that Jowett was so repelled by Darwinism. How is this repulsion to be explained? Was it merely that to the ear of the Stoical moralist, as well as to that of the devout Christian, the evolutionary beatitude, 'Blessed are the strong, for they shall prey on the weak,' rings with a jarring note? Probably this was one cause of Jowett's repulsion; but it was not, I think, the only cause. The word 'religion' was meant to include the higher morality as well as theology when I said not long ago that religion widens, while science narrows, the gulf between man and brute. The theological aspect of this question has already been touched on, for it has been contended that the view of the Divine goodness, on which alone can rest the 'trust that good will be the final goal of ill' to each individual man, will equally support the trust that good will be the final goal of ill to each individual moth or worm; and it has been mentioned that Jowett held, as most Theists would doubtless hold, this pressing home of logic to be extravagant. To the higher morality a somewhat similar mode of reasoning may be applied. The higher morality enjoins us to feel tender compassion for human suffering, and burning indignation against human wrong. But our sympathy is a limited quantity; and in order to be spread over all sentient beings it has to be beaten out very thin. The pity which a philanthropic cab-taker on a wet day feels for the drenched cabman is at once weakened if diluted with the thought of the lifelong toil and the frequent whippings of the cab-horse. And thus, if, with the melancholy Jaques, one for a moment

regards the deer as the lawful owners of their native
forests, or if, like a modern Xenophanes, one tries
to look on morality and religion from the point of
view of the lower animals, human progress will seem
to one a sorry achievement. It will appear that
philanthropists and reformers have indirectly stimulated the increase of population, and have thus
riveted the chains on the necks of the lower animals;
that more and more species that cannot, either living
or dead, minister to man's needs, are exterminated
as his rivals for food ; and that, to speak roughly,
we are nearing the point at which he will feel with
regard to his mute fellow-creatures that—

'They cannot live but to his shame, unless
It be to do him service.'

So, again, indignation at the wrongs inflicted by
man on man tends to be lessened if weighed in the
balance with the habitual treatment of the brutes by
man and by each other. Compared with their treatment of each other, the worst offences of man come
to be considered as a sort of animal survival, as
unsightly traces of the past—*priscæ vestigia fraudis*
—which development has not been able wholly to
obliterate. Thus, to put an extreme case, the ingratitude of Joash in slaying the son of Jehoiada
will appear, not perhaps less horrible, but certainly
less unnatural, if viewed side by side with the
undutiful requital which, through an instinct im-
planted by Nature herself, the young cuckoo accords
to the hospitality of its foster-parents. Hence, to a
cynical naturalist human ingratitude might appear

a regrettable but instructive example of atavism. Such a reversion to a primitive type (like the admonitory excrescence which, as if expressly designed to be a *memento originis,* so often plants itself on the human ear) may serve as proof that our paltry tenement of clay and nerves has not been adequately swept and garnished by natural selection —not wholly cleared of the leavings of our pre-human ancestors.*

Such are the stumbling-blocks with which the contemplation of the mutual relations of the lower animals may impede the pilgrim's progress towards an ethical paradise. I have called attention to those stumbling-blocks because they are not obvious. More obvious by far, but at the same time more important, are the difficulties connected with the treatment of the lower animals by man. Those difficulties are now exercising, and are likely more and more to exercise, an increasingly disturbing influence on ethical speculation; and, what is more to the point, I can record at first hand their disturbing influence on Jowett. A Greek sage has remarked that a man can say his say once, but not twice (δὶς δὲ οὐκ ἐνδέχεται). So I will venture, instead of recasting, to quote with additions some

* The hero of ' Maud,' after resolving to leave the world to its own devices, applies the queer goings on of the lower animals as a salve to his uneasy conscience :

' For Nature is one with rapine, a harm no preacher can heal ;
  The mayfly is torn by the swallow, the sparrow spear'd by
    the shrike,
  And the whole little world where I sit is a world of plunder
    and prey.'

sentences of my own which appeared in former articles, and which substantially represent the argument which I stated both to Pattison and to Jowett. In justice to myself, I should explain that I laid it before those distinguished men in no captious spirit, but because in my youth I was seriously troubled by Mill's astounding proposition that morality is bound to seek the greatest happiness of the greatest number of sentient beings. My contention was and is as follows:

'Mill insists that the Utilitarian principle should be applied not to man only, but to the entire sentient universe; and certainly it is less easy to show that the principle ought not to be so extended than that, if so extended, it might involve a *reductio ad euthanasiam*. May it not be argued that, from the philozoic point of view, the existence of the human race is altogether a mishap?* Does the unconstitutional monarchy of man minister to "the greatest happiness of the greatest number" of sentient beings, including earwigs and animalcules —including, let me add, hunted foxes, skinned eels, and vivisected guinea-pigs? We rightly condemn slavery, and we rightly think vegetarianism ridiculous; but a pitiless logician

---

* An ingenious poet has represented the squinancywort as lamenting that, after she had flourished for ages in peace, her *otium cum dignitate* was torn from her by the human oppressor. She is now liable to be plucked, and, worse still, she is called by a name which she regards as an insult! She concludes in a more cheerful tone:

'Yet there is hope:
I have seen
Many changes since life began;
Web-footed beasts have been
(Dear beasts!) and gone,
Being part of some wider plan:
Perhaps in His infinite mercy God will remove this—Man!'

might ask : *Why is it worse to domesticate our thousandth cousin than to kill and eat our millionth?* The argument, commonly employed by uncompromising utilitarians, that, as a matter of fact, we should never dream of keeping sheep and oxen alive except for our own ends, is practically identical with the argument which used to be employed in defence of slavery. If we loved all sentient beings as ourselves, should we not wish all alike to partake of our gratuitous beneficence? Moreover, the argument in question cannot be applied to the case of wild sentient beings, great or small. Mill's view of utilitarianism is hardly reconcilable with the use of insecticide powder. In brief, might not a cynic, weighing human joys and sorrows in the balance against the joys and sorrows of the entire animal kingdom, satirize our morality as a mere *égoisme à l'humanité?* *

In my 'Recollections of Pattison' I have mentioned that, when confronted with arguments of this sort, the Rector took refuge in good-humoured scepticism. He even relished the arguments, for they seemed to him to afford one among many proofs that the principle of rigid Stoicism may be pressed to absurd conclusions, and that the logic of martyrdom has a flaw in it. He doubtless thought that high ethical ideals have, for practical purposes, a positive and definite value, but that, when pressed by analysis, they disappear. Very different was the view taken by Jowett. On my asking him whether Mill's view, as expounded by me, did not seem logical, he answered, with some warmth, that it seemed to him very irrational. His excited voice and manner showed that the whole subject was dis-

* See 'Stones of Stumbling' (W. Rice), pp. 164-167, and 'Safe Studies' (W. Rice), pp. 231, 232.

tasteful to him. The region was evidently one
which lay outside the range of his ordinary mental
processes and appliances; and he was as bewildered
as an ant shorn of its antennæ. To me, he showed
the greatest sympathy and concern—the more so,
perhaps, because he seemed to be afraid that I was
taking leave of my senses. He hinted at a fear that
I might turn vegetarian. Then, on my stating my
views more clearly, he exclaimed, with evident relief:
'Oh! I understand it now—it merely is that you
are under the dominion of logic.' Of course, Jowett
was too righteous a man not to be merciful to beasts.
A quaint example of his tenderness to them has been
mentioned to me by a kinswoman of Pattison. The
Rector—thinking, perhaps, with Charles I., that
cats and parliaments grow curst with age — had
doomed a mother cat, which had long been domesti-
cated in his house, to be supplanted by one of her
daughters. But the decree was communicated to
Jowett, who seems to have thought that the principle
of the Fifth Commandment should govern our dealings even with cats. Might not so seductive a
maxim as *juniores priores* spread its infection from
feline to human relations? At the Master's entreaty
the claims of age and intimacy were preferred to the
playful attractiveness of youth.

The warning not to fall under the dominion of
logic was one frequently given by Jowett to his
pupils. What did he exactly mean by the phrase,
and under what circumstances did he wish them, as
it were, to spike logic? Probably he never formu-

lated a distinct answer to such questions; but his
general view is tolerably clear. Professor Henry
Smith, who, outside the domain of physical science,
cherished the same voluntary vagueness* that
characterized Jowett, once told me that Guizot, after
saying that St. Augustine forbore to press his
principles to their conclusions, praised this forbear-
ance, and Smith praised Guizot for praising it.†
I have not verified the passage in St. Augustine,
but I should doubt whether his spiking of logic was
of the same kind as Jowett's. The saint probably
meant to warn human reason to stick to its own
province, and not to trespass on the kingdom of God.
Jowett had, sometimes at any rate, an idea quite
different from this. At such times his idea probably
was that most ethical assumptions are not strictly
correct, and that, therefore, the more logically we
reason from these assumptions, the more certainly
will the initial error (like a stitch dropped in knitting)
vitiate the whole process. Such a view necessarily
implies something of what the French call *scepticisme*
—a quality which consists rather in ethical and
philosophical than religious scepticism, and which,

* Freeman, who took an extreme line with regard to the
Bulgarian atrocities, appears to have thought Henry Smith
somewhat lukewarm on this subject, and, when asked to support him in his election for Parliament, he replied that Smith
ought rather to sit in the Turkish Parliament as member for
Laodicæa.

† Guizot's words are curious. Speaking of the Pelagian
controversy, he says: ' La supériorité d'esprit de St. Augustin
le· sauva en cette occasion des erreurs ou l'eût précipité la
logique, et il fut inconséquent précisément à cause de sa haute
raison.'

moreover, serious French writers do not disavow. For example, even so earnest a moralist as Scherer ascribes this sort of scepticism to his friend Sainte-Beuve, and also, by implication, to himself. Thus, when he says, 'La vie exige des ménagements, j'allais dire des ruses,' his meaning must be interpreted by the light of the following sceptical utterance of his : ' L'humoriste n'en veut pas autrement à la nature humaine de repondre si peu à un idéal *arbitraire peut-être après tout.*'

Jowett's defiance of logic is in part due to a similar scepticism. But the word *scepticism* has an evil sound to English ears, and Jowett shared in the national repugnance to it. More than thirty years ago an article appeared in the *Saturday Review*, bitterly condemning the bigots who refused to increase his salary, but containing some such sentence as, 'Mr. Jowett seems to us to revel in doubt and scepticism.' Jowett spoke to me about the article, and, accustomed as I was to hear him described as the most sceptical of men, I was surprised to find how much annoyed he was by the charge being brought against him. To Pattison, on the other hand, such a charge would have caused no uneasiness whatever. It is probable, therefore, that in this respect the standpoints of the two men were less far asunder in reality than in appearance. Pattison was consciously not very unlike what Jowett was half consciously. Each of them dealt summarily with inconvenient ethical knots, while Jowett tried to persuade himself that he was untying them.

I am reminded of a famous controversy in Queen Anne's reign, wherein Addison and Steele took up opposite sides. 'It seems to us,' says Macaulay, 'that the premises of both the controversialists were unsound, that, on those premises, Addison reasoned well and Steele ill, and that consequently Addison brought out a false conclusion, while Steele blundered on the truth.' If, on the principle here indicated, ethical disputants could roughly be divided into Addisons and Steeles, Jowett's sympathy would have been on the side of the Steeles. Pattison's sympathy would have been on the side neither of the Addisons nor of the Steeles. He would have wished philosophers to follow the rule which has been laid down by Pascal, and which is especially noteworthy as coming from that anti-Jesuitical moralist : 'Il faut avoir une pensée de derrière et juger de tout par là, en parlant cependant comme le peuple.'

It was, indeed, unfortunate for Jowett that his sallies against logic often reached the ears of persons who had no notion of the source whence his severity had arisen. He was, in reality, combating that grim spectre of *narrow* logic whose haunt is in the abode of pedants. But to those pedants themselves, and to all whose eyes were holden that they could not see the ungainly apparition, the exorcist's gaze must have seemed idly bent on the air,

'And his vain words malicious mockery.'

Such vain words were attributed to him when he was reported to have said that he wished to see 'a desolating scepticism spread over the logic schools.'

And the report had at least verisimilitude, as some of his authentic sayings will show. Dean Fremantle tells me that, the question being discussed whether logic is a science or an art, he heard Jowett say: 'It is neither a science nor an art, but a dodge.' I acquired the knack, when I had to read essays to Jowett, of bringing into them now and then a reference to his favourite theories. Accordingly, in an essay on the province of logic, I said that the use of logic is 'less for the discovery of truth than for the detection of error, and less for the detection of error than for its exposure'; and from Jowett's strong expression of approval I saw that I had hit off his view exactly.

He once spoke to me about Buckle's assertion that the English mind is, in the main, inductive, and the German mind deductive. He said, on the authority of a scientific friend, that this statement is absurd; if Buckle had been accustomed to perform scientific experiments, he would have known that the inductive and deductive processes are commonly combined. To me this reasoning seems inconclusive. If induction and deduction are mutually dependent, so also are thought and language. And yet an able thinker is often a clumsy and obscure writer, and a clear and attractive writer is often a shallow thinker. And, in like manner, though induction and deduction are commonly intertwined, this is no reason why one mind, and, indeed, one science, should not be in the main inductive, and another mind and another science in the main deductive.

While praising Mill's 'Logic,' he told me that he wished that the author had broken off completely from formal logic. He seems to have cared less for Mill's later works. The peculiarities of some of those works he explained as most of us explain them. Most of us have long since come to the conclusion that to Mill might be applied the quaint remark which Herodotus made about Candaules of Lydia: he was madly 'in love with his own wife' (ἠράσθη τῆς ἑωυτοῦ γυναικός). Yet, however strongly Jowett may have shared this judgment and regretted the philosopher's uxoriousness, he yet regarded with grave disquietude the intellectual revolution which occurred some thirty years ago, the revolution by which Mill was dethroned at Oxford, and Hegel the German reigned in his stead.* Concerning Jowett's peculiar attitude towards German thought in general, and Hegelianism in particular, a few words must suffice.

When I went up to Oxford, it was reported that a former Rector of Lincoln had expressed a wish, in a University sermon, that 'German theology and German literature were at the bottom of the German Ocean.' It can hardly be doubted that, if the good

* A singular criticism on Mill's 'Logic' was made in my hearing by the late Rev. W. E. Jelf. That famous Censor of Christ Church complained that Mill, in his classification of modes of existence, did not refer to the change wrought in infants by Baptism. Mr. Jelf might plausibly and consistently have maintained that Baptism introduces the most important of all factors into human life. And yet I suspect that Jowett would have regarded him as 'under the dominion of logic,' with a vengeance! So hard it is for the two hostile parties to find any common ground.

Rector's real wish (or that of his spiritual descendants) could have taken effect, Jowett's writings, if not their author, would have been included in the general submersion. For, in my Oxford days, Jowett was considered as the representative of German heresy at Oxford. I certainly entertained this view; and especially I should have thought that the voluntary vagueness of which I have spoken would have placed him in sympathy with Hegel.* What he said to me about Hegel confirmed me in this opinion. At the time of our conversation my own knowledge on the subject was chiefly derived from the lines (written by Mansel) which satirize Germany as

> ' The land which produced one Kant with a K
> And many Cants with a C;
> Where Hegel taught to his profit and fame
> That something and nothing are one and the same,
> The absolute difference never a jot being
> 'Twixt having and not having, being and not being;
> But wisely declined to extend his notion
> To the finite relations of thalers and groschen.'

Jowett tried to explain to me what amount of truth is contained in this satire. He made me under-

---

* It has always seemed to me a happy thought of a recent romancist, when introducing a character which was clearly meant for Jowett, to represent that character as wishing that an obscure utterance ascribed to our Lord by both the Clements had made its way into the canon of Scripture. The passage referred to is as follows: ' The Lord, being asked when His kingdom should come, said: "When two shall be one, and that which is without as that which is within, and the male with the female neither male nor female." ' Would not this passage have obtained admission if there had been a Gospel according to Jowett?

stand what Hegel did *not* mean. Borrowing, I think,
Hegel's own illustration, he said that Hegel did not
mean that having a horse is the same thing as not
having a horse. But what Hegel actually did mean
Jowett himself perhaps understood, but certainly did
not make me understand. The point, however, is,
that he seemed to speak with sympathy of Hegel.
Why, then, was he afterwards averse to Hegelianism?
To this question I reply with diffidence. They say
at Oxford that both Jowett and T. H. Green plunged
into the whirlpool of German metaphysics, that
Green was permanently engulfed, but that Jowett
at last made his escape. I therefore conjecture
that, if Jowett seemed to me in some sort to cling
to Hegel, the reason may have been that at that
time he had not reached *terra firma*. Likewise, when
I was at Oxford, the Newmanite movement had
not quite passed away. Jowett probably regarded
Hegelianism as a less evil than Newmanism—indeed,
as an antidote to Newmanism. He also probably
regarded it as a less evil than Positivism, and he
knew that towards Positivism I myself was inclined.

I think it was in the conversation just referred to
that I praised Comte's hierarchy of the sciences;
whereto he rejoined that Hegel had also done good
service to science. I doubt, however, whether he
really rated Hegel more highly than Comte. A
friend writes to me: 'Once when I came back from
a holiday and told him [Jowett] I had been reading
Hegel, he said, "It's a good thing to have read
Hegel, but now that you've read him, I advise you

to forget him again."' In fact, he had no great liking
for science, or, indeed, any toleration of the truly
catholic—I had almost spelt the word with a capital
letter—claims which science has begun to put
forward. He seemed to think that the men of
science are now as likely to take too much upon
them as the sons of Levi or their modern counter-
parts ever were. 'Depend upon it,' he once said,
' scientific men have préjudices of their own quite as
much as other people.' One cause of his strong
opposition to the Positivists may have been the way
in which they make science their prop. Another
cause may have been his dissent from them as to
the primitive form of religion. In an essay that I
read to him, I referred to the controversy as to
whether the first men 'were cannibals and bar-
barians, or whether they lived in a golden age of
primæval simplicity' 'I don't believe that either
view is right,' interrupted Jowett. In another essay
I spoke of fetichism as the earliest form of religion.
Jowett cut me short by declaring that comparative
philology made against that view. Surely he must
afterwards have learnt that the point of time to
which comparative philology reaches back is far
later than the beginning of human society, while, on
the other hand, the Stone Age bears emphatic testi-
mony to the ascent of man. Altogether, it is not
easy to see why, as he liked Mill's logic, he so
disliked Positivism.* Perhaps, however, he let the

* I will remark in passing that, on my asking him what he
thought of the discussion between Mill and Mansel as to the

cat out of the bag when he once said to me, 'Positivism seems to me to lead to Atheism.' Obviously, a philosopher, pure and simple, would have concluded that, if Comte's principles are sound, and if they lead to Atheism, then—*So much the worse for Theism!* In other words, when Jowett spoke as he did, the philosopher in him was overmastered by the divine, or (let us say) by the moralist.

But whatever may have been Jowett's dislike of the Positive philosophy, no Positivist could have surpassed him in the scorn with which he sometimes spoke of Metaphysics. He quoted to me Voltaire's definition of Metaphysics as 'beaucoup de grand noms qu'on ne peut pas expliquer pour ce qu'on ne comprend pas,' a definition which cannot but recall the praise which its author bestowed on Zadig: 'Il savait de la métaphysique ce qu'on a su pendant tous les âges—c'est à dire, fort peu de chose.' Meeting me in the street after one of Mansel's Bampton Lectures, he turned upon me and said: 'How much have you learnt about the unconditional?' and passed on, laughing, without waiting for a reply. But the quaintest thing that he said was to a pupil who had been reading him an essay with a strong metaphysical flavour: 'It is remarkable what a fascination metaphysics seems to possess for the human mind. It is like falling in love. But

---

origin of the peculiar certainty which we ascribe to mathematical truths, he answered (not very relevantly): 'Isn't there another way of explaining the origin of our belief in mathematical truths? *We believed them in the first instance because we were taught them!*

you get over it after a time.'* Was it not Bishop Berkeley, himself our greatest metaphysician, who said of metaphysicians in general that they first kick up the dust and then complain that they cannot see? So thoroughly did Jowett concur with this weighty and unexpected admission, that he sometimes spoke slightingly even of Berkeley himself.

From metaphysics proper, the science of Absolute Being, I pass on to psychology, which is often confounded with metaphysics, but which rests on far surer foundations. Can Jowett in any sense be called a psychologist?†

We must remember that psychology is now closely connected with physiology; and that of the processes of physiology Jowett knew little or nothing; nay, even of the results of physiology and of its general aspects he knew far less than is known by many unscientific students. He, therefore, could not deal with psychology through the physiological method. But psychology has another method—the interrogation of consciousness. Buckle has argued (not perhaps very conclusively) that such interrogation has little value, for an object cannot be scientifically examined unless it remains passive; but the act of examination implies activity; therefore con-

---

* This reminds me of what Jowett is reported to have said in a sermon: 'The choice of a profession is like the choice of a wife. It does not so much matter what you choose, so long as you stick to it.'

† When I wrote this I did not know that the last edition of Jowett's 'Plato' contains an essay on psychology. I have thought it better to leave this paragraph in its original form, as containing my independent impression.

sciousness cannot properly examine itself; for how can it at the same moment be active as examiner and passive as examinee? I introduced this argument into an essay which I read to Jowett; and he, though scrupulously vigilant to point out everything that needed correction, left this statement unchallenged. Without pretending to attach any importance to this silence of his, I may say confidently that he took mental philosophy not very seriously in my younger days, and at the close of his life not seriously at all. And yet he was a student of philosophy. He thought at one time of writing a book on the early Greek philosophers. Talking to me on the subject, he said that some of those philosophers seemed to him 'not very interesting.' But he greatly admired Heraclitus, some of whose sayings certainly have a Hegelian flavour. Of Socrates and Plato he was, we all know, a worshipper. And, in a word, the maintenance of Greek philosophy in the position which it now holds in the schools of Oxford seemed to him essential to a high standard of University education. 'I don't often agree with Dr. Pusey,' he once said, 'but I agree with him in thinking that University training should be only in the best books. It is curious to compare this with the advice which he gave to Mr. (afterwards Lord) Bowen when the latter was going to the Bar: 'Read nothing but good books, and never anything that you don't like.' He knew that Bowen's professional duties would limit his time for desultory reading. It was, moreover, certain that Bowen would like only good books, while at the same time he, with his strong individuality, might have peculiar tastes; there were likely to be good books which he would not care for. I may illustrate this by mentioning that I heard Bowen say many years ago, 'I like " Transformation " better than all the " Adam Bedes " that come out in one's life. There is so much Idealism in it.' Doubtless he lived to take a juster view of George Eliot; but I think the remark worth quoting because the distinguishing note of Jowett and his disciples is thought to have been, not Idealism, but Scepticism. Plato and Aristotle he would clearly have included among the best books; and he was no less clearly desirous to guard the young against specializing their studies as early as studies are specialized in Germany—to guard them against taking, with beardless impetuosity, a vow of self-dedication to Accadian archæology or the examination of microbes! He was thus drawn into conflict with Brodie, who, as professor of chemistry, naturally wished to place men who had a turn for physical science under a scientific drill as soon as possible. But why did Jowett oppose himself to this wish? If, on his own showing, the study of metaphysics is unproductive, while that of science is so highly productive, why did he wish men to forsake the productive for the unproductive domain? Why should anyone

> ' on this fair mountain leave to feed,
> And batten on this moor ?'

To answer this question is not easy. Jowett

regarded as superficial the view expressed in Macaulay's 'Essay on Bacon,' the view that Philosophy should be thrust aside to make way for Science. Jowett probably thought that Macaulay, if he had not felt such an airy disdain for metaphysics, might have been saved from some of his metaphysical and theological errors.

Thus Macaulay in the 'Essay on Ranke' maintains that theology is not progressive. He admits, indeed, the progress of science may disintegrate a false theological system; but he does not at all see how much this admission involves. 'Every young Brahmin,' he says, 'who learns geography in our colleges, learns to smile at the Hindoo mythology. If Catholicism has not suffered to an equal degree from the Papal decision that the sun goes round the earth, this is because all intelligent Catholics now hold, with Pascal, that, in deciding the point at all, the Church exceeded her powers, and was, therefore, justly left destitute of that supernatural assistance which, in the exercise of her legitimate functions, the promise of her Founder authorized her to expect.' As a matter of fact, every argument that can be used to show that either the Bible or the Church had to accommodate its language to the scientific errors of its time could be equally used to show that the sacred books of the Hindoos were under the necessity of practising a similar accommodation. In particular, Macaulay asserts that Sir Thomas More 'had all the information on the subject [transubstantiation] that we have, or that, while the world lasts, any human being will have.' I asked Jowett whether he agreed with this statement. He replied in the negative. 'The belief in transubstantiation,' he said, 'is closely connected with the mediæval distinction between essence and accidents; the accidents of the consecrated bread and wine were held to be bread and wine, their essence was held to be the body and blood of Christ; but we now hold that substances which have all the sensible properties of bread and wine *are* bread and wine; thus, with the decline of mediæval metaphysics, the foundations of transubstantiation were undermined.'

Here, then, is one reason why Jowett wished the young to be trained in the use of metaphysical weapons; he thought that it was only by means of such weapons that the domain of metaphysics could be curtailed. Buckle used to maintain that the chief work of governments should now be to undo the work which former governments have done; and, with a like vehemence, Jowett once protested that the chief use of metaphysics is to get rid of metaphysics altogether. But this paradox did not represent his deliberate opinion. I lately talked on the subject to an intimate friend of Jowett, who generally agreed with him, and who has had great educational experience; and I asked him what he thought Jowett's deliberate opinion on the matter was. 'Personally,' he replied, 'I should say that the young ought to be disciplined in abstract thought, because through such discipline they acquire qualities which they could not acquire otherwise.' Though my friend spoke only for himself, he was clearly expressing the opinion held by Jowett and by some of his disciples. More or less persistently Jowett and some of his disciples have thought that, in this and other lines of study, the activity (ἐνέργεια) which the study involves is more important than any result (ἔργον) which the activity is likely to achieve. If we carry this line of thought a little further, we are led to the scepticism of Renan or of the late Mr. Pearson. The answer to the Great Riddle never is but always to be guessed; but it is only through thinking it guessable and trying to guess it that we can keep our sympathies from being narrowed and the wings of our imagination from being clipped. And this is surely an unexhilarating and unstimulating conclusion. Mankind, it seems, is like a squirrel in a rotatory cage, vainly hoping to rise, but enticed by that vain hope, as it could not be enticed otherwise, to take the exercise needful for its health. So indissolubly, indeed, is our highest life bound up with limitless longings, if not with illusions, that we are tempted to exclaim · ' E vanitate sanitas; e sanitate vanitas !'*

* Clough, who was the poet of devout scepticism, as Matthew Arnold was the poet of devout unbelief, has thrown this peculiar mode of feeling into the short poem called 'Life is Struggle,' in which he laments that human effort is often

> ' absurd and vain !
> O, 'tis not joy, and 'tis not bliss,
> Only it is precisely this
> That keeps us still alive.'

In a somewhat similar spirit Scherer speaks of the ' agitation sans but qui constitue la comédie humaine.'

In this and some other matters I am on my guard against confidently ascribing opinions to Jowett, for his mind seemed often to be in a state of flux. Some of his opinions varied, not merely from decade to decade or from year to year, but from conversation to conversation. Thus, when I went to Oxford fresh from my Tory home, I understood Jowett to advocate Universal Suffrage and the Ballot, which latter was then thought a frightful heresy. My impression was confirmed by one of our Balliol Scholars, who told me that on one occasion, having said in Jowett's presence that he thought secret voting un-English, he was cut short by the question, ' Do you think bribery and intimidation English ?' On the other hand, one of Jowett's Radical friends told me that he believed him to be far more Conservative than I supposed. On further inquiry, I found that Jowett sometimes spoke differently to different persons, but in doing this he was, not only not an *assentator*, but rather what may be called *dissentator*. Goethe has remarked that, whenever we hear an opinion strongly expressed in conversation, our impulse is to take the opposite side. A man of the world tries to control this impulse, but Jowett was not a man of the world; and also perhaps the habit of correcting, if not of contradicting, which he acquired as a college tutor, had become with him a second nature. This aggressive sincerity of his assuredly does not lessen our esteem for him; but does it not militate against his claim to be regarded as an ideal philosopher? What shall we say of his

inconsistency ? That somewhat misleading word
has, even when applied to purely speculative
matters, at least two significations. It denotes
sometimes inconsecutiveness in reasoning, and
sometimes inconstancy in opinion. I have already
remarked that a consecutive reasoner Jowett was
not. Much as he admired Plato, he neither pos-
sessed nor coveted that 'wonderful hardihood in
speculation' which Macaulay ascribes to Plato,
'who shrank from nothing to which his principles
led.' And we now see that Jowett was not consistent in the other sense. He did not always stick
to his guns, or, rather, he did not always point
them in the same direction. It is true that Sir
Henry Maine speaks of consistency as a much
overrated virtue. But in saying this he is speaking
of steadfastness of opinion from youth to age, and
not from conversation to conversation.* Thus,
then, Jowett was inconsistent in a twofold sense;
and on that account he hardly seems to me to
deserve the praise accorded to him by his friendly
critic whom I have cited, the praise of being unrivalled in the art of seeing through and through an
abstract question. But I think we may perceive
what the merit of Jowett was which his critic had in

* Renan, like Jowett, made a virtue of inconsistency. He
even declared, in his odd way, that he liked to express a great
variety of opinions, because one of his opinions so expressed
had a good chance of being correct. This is like saying that a
watch which stops is better than a watch which goes perfectly
well but is a second wrong, because the watch which stops will
be exactly right for one moment in every twelve hours, whereas
the watch which is a second wrong will never be exactly right.

his mind. The Master, as the French would say, had the good qualities belonging to his defects. Through his habit of taking a link of a chain of reasoning by itself and detaching it from the link before and the link after, he could both examine that link better and describe it better. Hence it was that his *aperçus* were often brilliant and brilliantly expressed. One of his ablest friends, referring to him as a sort of prose-poet, once remarked to me that 'poetry may solve the riddle of the universe, but philosophy and science never will.' This paradox is open to very obvious objections, and, at best, it recalls what, I think, Muretus says of Plato : 'Non absurde dicunt qui illum dicant poetice philosophari.' Such a poetical philosophizer was Jowett ; and the habit of mind thus acquired gave, as many persons would think, to his mystical utterances a spontaneous and lifelike vigour which the clearly-defined utterances of Pattison and Freeman generally lack, just as it is to many persons not merely pleasanter, but more helpful, more healthily educative, to see a butterfly flitting from flower to flower than to see the same butterfly named and pinned in an entomological collection.

The natures of Freeman and Jowett could hardly fail to jar one another. A good story is told at Oxford that, when Jowett was Vice-Chancellor, some question of University politics arose, involving a historical difficulty. It was thought expedient to consult Freeman. Whereupon Jowett, instead of sending a note, told his servant to

6

ask Professor Freeman to come to see him. The historian, forecasting from his irregular summons some grave and immediate disaster, straightway forsook his studies and made haste to call on the Vice-Chancellor. But in the meantime the difficulty had been solved; and Jowett bowed out his visitor with the brief explanation: 'Thank you, Freeman, I've found out what I wanted, good-bye.' They say that Freeman was sore displeased, and that his displeasure was not hidden—οἰκότα λέγοντες ('saying what is likely,') as Herodotus would have phrased it. Whether this story is true or false, it should be remembered that Jowett at the close of his life had, not the trials of a monarch, but the worst trials of what I will venture to call a *donarch*. He must, in fact, unless he was more than human, have combined the occasional inconsiderateness of the absorbed scholar with something of the autocratic pedantry which is the besetting weakness of a chief among dons.

In illustration of the antagonism between Jowett and Freeman, I will instance a criticism of Jowett's, which, though not picturesque, is characteristic of the author, and is, moreover, curious because Freeman either could not or would not understand it. In an article on Jowett's 'Thucydides,' he remarks: 'Mr. Jowett gets beyond me when he says that in moral and philosophical speculations "we have not so completely got rid of the 'subjective' element as we are sometimes inclined to imagine."' This utterance, I say, is especially characteristic of Jowett. One reason of this is that it has a flavour of the half-scepticism, half acknowledged, which leavened his whole character. It also has Jowett's peculiar indefiniteness, which, indeed, is what repelled Freeman. But it is through this very indefiniteness that the utterance is many-sided; and that the more it is turned over, the more aspects it seems to present. When it is considered in reference to history, it seems to be pitched in the same key as a passage in 'Faust':

'Die Zeiten der Vergangenheit
Sind uns ein Buch mit sieben Siegeln;
Was ihr den Geist der Zeiten heisst,
Das ist im Grund der Herren eigner Geist,
In dem die Zeiten sich bespiegeln.'

The picture presented to us by the irrevocable past is faded. We try to restore it; but the restoration is never quite complete:

'Neque amissos colores
Lana refert mendicata fuco.'

In other words, 'the subjective element' which we supply never quite replaces the objective element which is lost.

Especially is this subjective element apparent in the moral judgments that we pass on bygone days. I think it was Tennyson who once said that 'every man imputes himself.' It is at least equally true that every age, every state of society, imputes itself —judges, that is, every other age and state of society by its own standard. When we pour out the vials of our wrath on ancient misdoings—on slavery, for example, or persecution, or assassination—we are not, to be sure, quite as indignant as we should be if such iniquities occurred among ourselves; but still, we do not let ourselves freely breathe the intellectual and moral atmosphere in which the iniquities throve; we impute our own age to some extent.* Why this is and must be so may be shown by an example, which will also show that the light thrown by morality on the past is not always what Bacon would have called a dry light. The giving and taking of bribes was perhaps thought as excusable in the time of Elizabeth as nepotism was thought in the days of my youth. But if a historian were to speak of Elizabethan bribery as indulgently as men of the world used to speak of Victorian nepotism, he would justly be censured as immoral. For history must never overlook the present needs of morality; and ordinary readers will not make full allowance for the difference of standards. If they are taught to condone Elizabethan and Jacobean bribery, they will be in danger of condoning Victorian bribery also. Charles Austin told me that at the beginning of this century a judge, passing sentence of death on a horse-stealer, said to the prisoner: 'You are sentenced to be hanged, not because you stole the horse, but in

* A well-known writer has lately 'imputed himself' by speaking with disdainful pity of Brutus for being so blind as not to see that assassination cannot permanently succeed. Are we sure that it never permanently succeeds? If we are, the lesson is a very unobvious one, and has been learnt only through a long historical experience. And to blame Brutus for not having had this experience is about as reasonable as it would be to blame him for not having won a great victory at Philippi by forestalling (as the Miltonic devils forestalled) the invention of gunpowder.

order that horses may not be stolen.' And, in like manner, it may be affirmed that Bacon, as Chancellor, is gibbeted by posterity, not because he took bribes, but in order that bribes may not be taken.

One or two more examples may be given, examples which will throw light on some other of Jowett's opinions. The convenient gift, so to say, of *metaphesying*—of prophesying after the event—has been unstintingly bestowed on the human race; and with this gift has arisen the desire to convert metaphecy into prophecy, and to attribute such prophecy to the worthies of the past. We thus impute ourselves, often unconsciously. Our estimate, for instance, of Charles I. and his followers should clearly be unaffected by events which they could not possibly foresee. The present reaction against Puritanism among the educated classes, and the dread of democracy which is growing up among large sections of those classes, these are events which the Cavaliers certainly could not have foreseen. Yet these changes dispose some of us to take the line of Matthew Arnold rather than the line of Macaulay, and to see good in the party of Falkland as well as in the party of Hampden.

Jowett had no love for Puritanism;* and his sympathy with democracy was perhaps, at bottom, as questionable as his sympathy with the Athanasian Creed. With this cast of mind did he never feel the

---

* I may mention that Jowett once read to me with impressive emphasis Wesley's famous diatribe against the fundamental doctrine of Calvinism.

cold shudder which many of us have felt at the thought of England dominated by the Roundheads? At all events he had a weakness for Charles I. I once told him that Charles Austin had said that, if the unfortunate King had been born in a private station, he would have been conspicuous as an accomplished and high-bred gentleman, 'something between Lord Derby and Lord Lansdowne.'* 'He would have been a great deal more religious than either,' rejoined Jowett, with a laugh. Did he mean to imply that to take theology quite seriously is a defect in a politician and may be a source of danger?

Especially were some of Jowett's friends startled by his sympathetic attitude towards Louis Napoleon and the Second Empire. The fear of democracy is now inducing some superannuated Liberals, and other *Liberals by courtesy*, to think that popular government is a kind of watch which sometimes goes wrong or even comes to a standstill, and that then a cunning craftsman is needed to alter the regulator or to put in new works altogether. Thus it is that hints are beginning to be dropped in unexpected quarters as to the occasional opportuneness of 'saviours of society.' But the indulgence felt by Jowett for one such saviour of society dated as far back as the *coup d'état*. An eminent friend of his tells me that, shortly after that audacious act had been carried out, he heard Jowett contend that there

---

* 'Safe Studies,' p. 216. He was speaking of Lord Derby, the Prime Minister, and of Lord Lansdowne, the Mæcenas of half a century.

had been a struggle for life and death between the popular leaders and the Prince-President: and the triumph of the popular leaders might, Jowett thought, have meant anarchy. Many years later, Jowett quite agreed with Arthur Stanley in wishing that a monument to the Prince Imperial could be put up in Westminster Abbey. That the heir of the great Napoleon should have died fighting on the English side was a piece of irony worthy of a Greek tragedy. Jowett thought that a memorial of so extraordinary a catastrophe would have an interest for posterity; and that in our great national collection of monuments—our *petrified history,* as I may call it—such a memorial would not be out of place.

Jowett's views may sometimes be illustrated by those of his ablest disciples. So I will mention that Bowen (about 1859) praised France as being then a great apostle of liberty, in that she helped to give the Italians the boon which she herself lacked. Reversing the praise bestowed by Byron on Venice, he might have described France as at that time

'Herself a slave, yet making many free.'

We have thus caught a glimpse of Jowett's view of democracy, and therefore indirectly of his view of progress. For democracy and progress are in a manner unequally joined together. So strongly has the current set in towards democracy that a consistent thinker, unless he expects the tide to turn, can hardly be distrustful about democracy without being uneasy about progress; while, on the other hand, as progress is beset by other dangers besides the danger from democracy, a man may be uneasy about progress even though he is a stanch democrat. We have seen that Jowett was distrustful of democracy, and therefore we should expect him to have been more than sceptical about progress. But we have also seen that he was not a consistent thinker : and he may, moreover, have thought that a change will come over the fortunes of democracy; so much so, indeed, that peradventure, after a periodic or continually accelerated recurrence of Reigns of Terror, democracy will at last be condemned by natural selection.* Is there, then, any reason to suppose that Jowett anticipated that 'ideal future of society' which Matthew Arnold declared to be the reality underlying the belief in the kingdom of heaven, and which, in the face of the forlorn prophecy of science, that our planet will be gradually frozen up, that too poetical critic so confidently foretold.† To the question whether Jowett did or

---

* Is there any likelihood that democracy will be thus condemned? A reply to this question is suggested by a remark of De Tocqueville. That great *conservateur malgré lui* has maintained that Europe, if parcelled out into federal republics after the American model, would probably support a larger population than at present, and in greater comfort; but that, if a single feudal monarchy were left among them, that monarchy might be able to impose its own will on the entire continent. In like manner, Renan, after the experience of the Franco-German War, prognosticated that, if (as he feared) the aristocratic organization of the army is impracticable in France, France exposes herself to the risk of being again conquered by the Germans, and that, sooner or later, again conquered she will be.

† Is it strange that Matthew Arnold should have felt, nay, have caressed, this unreasoning confidence? What can be

did not think such a millennium possible I am tempted to apply a passage of Tennyson :

> ' " Is there any hope ?"
> To which an answer pealed from that high land,
> But in a tongue no man could understand.'

Dean Fremantle assures me that Jowett seemed to him to be in general sanguine about progress, but that, towards the end of his Vice-Chancellorship, his physical exhaustion inclined him to political despondency. Jowett also sometimes spoke sanguinely to me. A statement made by Lord John Russell (about 1857), that he saw no reason why a nation should not remain great for ever, led to my asking Jowett whether he thought that the analogy of the decadence of the nations of antiquity obliged us to expect that modern nations will also decline. He answered that the analogy does not quite hold ; the great industrial development of some modern nations places them on a different footing from the ancient nations, whose population consisted chiefly of slaves. I spoke of the decline of some modern nations, such as Spain. He said that their decline seemed to him

---

more disheartening for an idealist whose hope of heaven has grown dim than to lose also the foretaste of an earthly paradise, and to become convinced that, not men only, but planets, have their maturity and decay, and are even as the grass of the field ?—

Οἵη μὲν φυλλῶν γενέη, τοιήδε καὶ ἀ σ τ ρ ῶ ν.

Is the time ever to come when a degenerating and dwindling humanity will feel a mingled pride and self-loathing as it looks back on its past, and as it exclaims, with the ghost of Remus : ' Cernite qualis sim qui modo talis eram ' (To have been what I have been, being what I am) ?

rather relative than absolute; they have been out-
stripped by other nations in the race. He disliked
the pessimism of Carlyle. But he seems to have
admired Carlyle's 'Heroes,' with the exception of
Goethe. Shortly after Carlyle's death reference was
made to Proctor's statement that it was not impossible that, about the year 1897, a comet might
strike the sun, and for a few days raise the sun's
temperature just so much as to cause the destruction
of all animal life on the earth. 'How pleased,' said
Jowett, 'would Mr. Carlyle have been to hear this if
he had been alive!' Jowett asked more than once
what lasting effect Carlyle had produced on the
world. Some one quoted Carlyle's injunction, 'Do
the work that lies nearest to thee.' 'That had been
said before,' rejoined Jowett. Charles Austin told
me that he doubted whether the French had really
gained anything by the Revolution. Jowett, on my
repeating this remark to him, declared that Austin
was simply wrong, as statistics proved the French
peasant to be better off now than in the last century.
It is, however, probable that what Austin meant to
affirm was that France is politically weaker now
than she was under the old *régime,* and that she is,
therefore, exposed to the perils to which political
weakness is liable. Jowett spoke to me about the
conservative tendency of old age (that tendency
which Goethe has affirmed to be universal), and he
said that he was doing his utmost to struggle against
it. He attributed this propensity to the fact that old
men feel that they occupy a less prominent place

than they used to do. Surely a more obvious, and also a more creditable, explanation may be drawn from the nervous enfeeblement of old men, from the fact that they are 'afraid of that which is high, and fears are in the way,'* and that they continually feel more and more that their old modes of thought and conduct, as well as their old friends, are sinking into oblivion. Such a view of the unsanguine and let-alone quality of old age seems to be indicated in the famous lines:

> 'The clouds that gather round the setting sun
> Do take a sober colouring from an eye
> That hath kept watch o'er man's mortality.'

Jowett went on to say that, if human life were ten years longer, the world would come to a standstill. He doubtless meant that this evil result would ensue if life were thus lengthened without youth being correspondingly lengthened. Unhappily, such a result is that which medical improvement is bringing about. And, indeed, this is one of the reasons assigned by that Cassandra of Cassandras, Mr. Pearson, for his foreboding that the human race collectively, as well as an undue proportion of the individuals of which it will hereafter be composed, is fated. to count among dotards 'senes in vivaria missos,' and to waste away in lethargic decrepitude.

In the instance just given, Jowett's optimism verges on pessimism, or, let us say, his *bonism* verges on *malism*. Other and more distinct malistic utterances of his will be subjoined; but, before

* Eccles. xii. 5.

entering on these, it may be well to show how his self-contradiction may be explained. I mentioned that he spoke of the decline of nations as being often more relative than absolute. May not a like remark be in some measure applied to human progress? Scherer, in speaking of Mr. Gladstone, says that he inclines more and more to Radicalism, and that Radicalism

' n'est autre chose que l'application de l'absolu à la politique. Le malheur veut que la politique soit précisément ce qu'il y a de plus relatif au monde, de sorte que le radicalisme n'est bon qu'à faire des révolutions et, en temps ordinaire, risque per-pétuellement de mettre les institutions en avance sur les mœurs.'

He doubtless means that, in seeking to carry popular measures, it is hardly possible to avoid enunciating principles, as universally applicable, which are in reality applicable, at most, only to advanced states of society; and thence arises the habit of ascribing an absolute and a scientific character to mere working hypotheses, and even to what may be called *working fictions*. An instance of such working fictions is shown in the broad assertions that are sometimes made as to the extreme happiness of some states of society and the extreme misery of others. A view which draws so broad a contrast between different states of society can hardly be maintained. Rather should we maintain that what Rochefou-cauld has affirmed of individuals may be at least as truly applied to states of society: they are seldom or never either as happy or as unhappy as they are commonly thought to be. Whence has arisen the exaggeration in what is commonly thought about them? One cause of that exaggeration seems to be that men are apt to ignore the extreme adaptiveness of human nature, and in doing so they also ignore the extent to which they judge of all things by comparison. A daughter of Methuselah who had been snatched away in beauty's bloom ere completing her second century would have stirred the deepest compassion; but we should now rather say that, with so protracted an adolescence, she had not a bad time of it! A like idea is well expressed by Moses Primrose: 'We are not to judge of the feelings of others by what we might feel in their place. However dark the habitation of the mole to our eyes, yet the animal itself finds the apartments sufficiently lightsome.' The above saying of the ingenious son of the Vicar of Wakefield amounts to this: the savage is not, any more than the mole, so much to be pitied as we are apt to think, for not being an Englishman. No one is truly *infortunatus sua si mala nescit.*

The point may be stated in another way. The fact that, the more men get, the more they want, has enabled them to get more and more, and is therefore a blessing; but the blessing is not without drawbacks, for a chronic state of wanting means chronic uneasiness. In fact, the progressive desires to which civilization owes so much are only another name for retrogressive satisfaction. This may furnish a clue to what seems a very mysterious anomaly.

Since the time of the early Cæsars at least a score of results have been achieved by civilization—achievements ranging from the triumphs of Catholicism to the invention of railways and the higher education of women—each of which is referred to as an unspeakable boon. Now really, if we try to add up the presumable effects of even a few of these unspeakable boons, we begin to think that the Roman Empire must have been worse than a purgatory, and that, on the other hand, during the last few centuries our regenerated planet must have been blossoming into an earthly paradise. Great, therefore, is our disappointment when we learn that Gibbon, and, I believe, Curtius, have favoured the opinion that under some of the Cæsars the civilized world was at least as happy as it has ever been since. Tennyson, too, was clearly balancing the ancient against the modern world when he put the saddening query:

' Rome of Cæsar, Rome of Peter, which is crueller, which is
    worse ?'

Jowett would, I suspect, have preferred—have felt bound to prefer—the Rome of Peter to the Rome of Cæsar, and the Rome of King Humbert to either. But would he have expected the improvement to go on? In 1860 he repeated to me approvingly a saying of Tennyson that ' things are going quite fast enough.' Things have not stood still since 1860, and it may be surmised that he ultimately came to think, as Tennyson certainly did, that things have lately been going much too fast. So again, I once, with the self-confidence of youth, quoted to him the

Homeric saying that 'We boast that we are much better than our fathers '—

'Ημεῖς τοι πατέρων μέγ' ἀμείνονες εὐχόμεθ' εἶναι.

He replied that, whenever he heard that line, he felt a wish to oppose to it another passage from Homer, the passage in which Diomed is reproached with being inferior to his father in deeds, though superior to him in words :

Τοῖος ἔην Τυδεύς Αἰτώλιος ἀλλὰ τὸν υἱὸν
Γείνατο εἷο χέρεια μάχῃ, ἀγορῇ δέ τ' ἀμείνω.

On the whole, then, after putting side by side the bonistic and the malistic sayings of Jowett, and weighing them against one another by the light of our general impression of him, we may roughly consider the question : What did he think of the value of civilization and of its future ? I will not again employ the metaphor of the rotating squirrel; for that metaphor, while it seems to express Jowett's view of the course of metaphysical inquiry, does not fully express his view of the course of civilization. Goethe, we all know, said that civilization moves, not in a circle, but in a spiral. To complete this metaphor, let us suppose the spiral to be horizontal like a corkscrew laid flat on a table. Human society, travelling along the line of such a spiral, has its ups and downs, but is continually going forward in a definite direction. This metaphor, I think, fairly expresses Jowett's view. At all events, in times of depression (or of candour) he would have admitted that the harvest reaped by civilized men bears no

sort of proportion to the labour which their fore-
fathers bestowed on sowing the seed. This will
appear more plainly when some other of Jowett's
sayings, especially his sayings about democracy,
have been recorded.

I was referring to Jowett, and referring to him
advisedly, when I said many years ago:

' We have known very able men who, in their feelings, were
tenacious of the past, and who, in small matters, gave way to
those feelings—who, for example, were made quite uncom-
fortable if their seat was changed at the dinner-table; while
yet, when any important question arose, they reasoned themselves into being reformers.'*

This Conservatism of feeling must be borne in
mind even when we are considering the Liberalism
which marked Jowett in the earlier days of my
acquaintance with him. It was then that I asked
him about a strike in which the workmen seemed to
me to make unreasonable demands. He replied
rather paradoxically: ' Those demands are so utterly
unreasonable that they remind me of the inarticulate
cry of intelligent animals. Let us hope that when
the men get the franchise they will speak and act
more wisely.' Long after this Dean Fremantle
asked him what he thought of arbitration between
employers and workmen. 'Depend upon it,' he
replied, ' the working man knows best where the
shoe pinches.' In a more Conservative mood, he
said to another pupil: ' The working men have had

* 'Safe Studies,' p. 174.

a hard time of it hitherto. I am afraid that some
day they may get more than their due'—more, he
of course meant to say, than will be conducive to
the strength and stability of the country.

When I was an undergraduate, I heard a young
man, who belonged to the ruling classes, express, in
Jowett's presence, strong disgust at the way in which
the sceptre was departing from those classes. Jowett
replied that it was simply impossible that the government of the country should continue in the hands of
a small number of families, and added: 'A man
who lives, as you do, in the first society in the
country, should remember that there is as much
vulgarity in thinking too much of social advantages
as in affecting to despise them.' Nevertheless, he
once said to me that he hoped that, in spite of
democratic changes, some remains of the old feudal
feeling will still survive. He wished to keep up the
House of Lords, and even wished the Bishops to
retain their seats in it. 'It keeps them out of
mischief,' he said with a laugh.* He remarked that
the landed gentry are generally kind to the poor,
and he liked the agricultural labourer as a class.
He astonished me by saying that, on the other hand,
the young coxcomb whom one sometimes sees behind
the counter of a shop 'makes one's whole soul

---

* Jowett told a story of a parishioner who, when his new
vicar brought politics into his sermons, exclaimed: 'Let him
stick to doctrine. *That can do no harm.*' This recalls the
rejoinder made by the Catholic Radicals in Ireland when they
were commanded by the Pope to submit loyally to England:
'As much theology from Rome as you please, but no politics!'

nauseate.'* He was doubtless provoked into speaking thus by some remembered experience of that objectionable sort of person; but he would hardly have used the expression at all if he had wished to see the old-fashioned rustic educated out of existence.

The late Professor of Chemistry, Sir B. Brodie, himself as unorthodox as might be, said of the aggressive anti-orthodoxy of the late Rev. Baden Powell: 'I don't like to see a man throwing stones at the house in which he lives.' My father had the same sort of feeling about aristocratic Radicals. So strongly did he at one time distrust Lord Stanley (the late Lord Derby) in particular, that he might have applied to him the remark which George Eliot made about Harold Transome: 'The utmost enjoyment of his own advantages was the solvent that blended pride in his family and position with the adhesion to changes that were to obliterate tradition, and melt down enchased gold heirlooms into plating for the egg-spoons of "the people."' I asked Jowett how he regarded men of this stamp. 'At all times,' he answered, 'there have been born aristocrats who

---

* 'A tradesman behind his counter must have no flesh and blood about him, no passions, no resentment; he must be all soft and smooth; he must be a perfect, complete hypocrite, if he will be a complete tradesman.'—DEFOE. Charles Lamb says of this soulless animal 'that his customers are to be his idols; so far as he may worship idols, by allowance, he is to bow down to them, and worship them.' Contrast with this unflattering view of our middle classes the view taken by Voltaire. The English people he wittily compared to English beer. The highest stratum seemed to him mere froth; the lowest mere dregs; but all the rest he thought excellent.

have taken the popular side, partly, no doubt, from motives of ambition, but *partly also from a sense of right.*' Not, indeed, that his admiration for Lord Stanley was unqualified. I told him that Lord Stanley was reported to have said: 'My father would be a very clever man if he was not so frightfully ignorant.' Jowett returned sharply: 'If he ever becomes the equal of Lord Derby, he may think himself fortunate.' He was distinctly attracted by Lord Derby, and was amused by the good sayings ascribed to him. Some of these were repeated before him and by him, including, I think, the one about Lord Stanley coming in unusually good spirits into his father's presence. 'What's the news?' said his father, looking up from his game of billiards. 'Are you going to be married, or is Dizzy dead?' I mention this familiar story with its reference to Disraeli, because of the spell which seems at one time to have been cast over Jowett by that impressive and inscrutable personality. According to my father, and, as I understood, in his presence, Disraeli said that he was himself regarded by Lord Derby with a dislike ' worse than hate.' Though this assertion of Disraeli was doubtless a jocular hyperbole, he at any rate implied that he was not a favourite with his chief. And I may add that, at that time, he was by no means a favourite with my father or with the bulk of the country gentlemen.

Having thus early imbibed a prejudice against Disraeli, I was purposing to make a speech disparaging to him in the Oxford Union. On my

mentioning the fact to Jowett, he said: 'I won't
have you throw stones at Dizzy.' Afterwards he
saw something of Disraeli, who, indeed, had a
fascination for him not wholly unlike that which,
up to a certain point, Louis Napoleon had—the
fascination whereby a sensitive and imaginative
nature is drawn to a man of enigmatical character
who has achieved an extraordinary success. But
either Disraeli's influence over him waned, or else
the fascination of which I speak had in it an element
of repulsion. So I at least infer from a fragment
of a conversation with Jowett, the notes of which a
friend has shown me:

Friend.—' Do you like Dizzy's novels ?'
Jowett.—' Yes; very good novels. But I have not read
them all.'
F.—' Did you know Dizzy ?'
J.—' Yes. I did not like him much; he flattered a great
deal, and always talked for the sake of talking.'
F.—' He was very Jewish in many ways.'
J.—' He loved magnificence.'

In reading Renan's account of St. John the Divine,
I was reminded of Disraeli by a passage which runs,
if I remember rightly, as follows: ' Il entasse l'or.
Il a, comme tous les Orientaux, un goût immodéré
pour les pierres précieuses.' Another distinguished
man who, long hated by the Conservatives, won
their favour at the end of his life, was Brougham.
Jowett gave proof of his own Liberalism when he
said to me long ago: ' Brougham might have been
the first man in the country if he had not let him-

self be overcome by the blandishments of the aristocracy.'*

In thus recording some sayings of Jowett which more or less illustrate his view of democracy and progress, I have kept in reserve one saying of his which has a distinctive malistic flavour. He either originated or approvingly quoted the remark that 'Art is the bloom of decay.' To a somewhat similar effect, a great historian has said that art, in its relation to religion, is like painted glass in a cathedral : it dims the light, while it beautifies it. Unhappily, as nearly all old nations have had a season of artistic bloom and now have it not, it would seem to follow that in their case the flowering of the aloe is over, and they are themselves nigh to corruption.

It might have been thought that Jowett, thinking so ill of the social atmosphere in which art thrives,

* Shortly before the death of Brougham, of whom Mill had written hard things, I was so fortunate as to sit next Mill and the late Lord Lyttelton at breakfast with Mr. Gladstone. Mill playfully remarked what a good thing it would be if the elixir of life could be given to a few of the most eminent men of each generation; and both he and Lord Lyttelton agreed in naming Lord Brougham as a proper recipient of the potion. I suggested that the draught should be also taken by the old Lord Combermere, who had told my father that, but for the Prince Regent's opposition, Wellington would have put him in command of the cavalry during the Hundred Days. Both my hearers put me to silence, the one saying and the other implying that the veteran Lord Combermere was little better than a fool. The line thus taken by the scholarly saint and the saintly sage impressed me a good deal; it made me feel that intellectual men nearly always have more sympathy with intellectual, as opposed to moral, distinction than is commonly supposed, or than they themselves suppose. Was there not a friendship between Johnson and Beauclerc, and at least a semi-friendship between Jowett and Lord Westbury ?

must himself have set a low value on art. But such
was far from being the case. A former pupil, before
he had taken the irrevocable step into the impe-
cunious blessedness of matrimony, consulted Jowett
as to what he should do with his superfluous cash.
'He told me,' the pupil writes, 'to get some first-
rate Rembrandt and other etchings, and I have
always been grateful to him for his advice.' Jowett
had also a taste for a certain kind of music. A lady
tells me that he often asked her for old-fashioned
music, especially for three songs: Haydn's 'My
mother bids me bind my hair,' Bishop's 'Should he
upbraid,' and 'She never told her love.' He also
often begged her for Corelli, and, on her asking the
reason, answered: 'I can't say, unless it is because
my mother liked it.' The same lady tells me that
the Master, when his sister died, said mournfully:
'The college must be my family now.' I am assured
that he once declared that, if some benignant fairy
had promised him the highest distinction in any
single line that he liked to name, he would have
chosen to excel, not as a scholar, a statesman, or
philosopher, but as a musical composer. Poetry
must also be regarded as a form of art; and Jowett
was a great admirer of some poets, and was, indeed,
more than enthusiastic about Shakespeare. In illustration of what may fairly be called his Shakespear-
olatry, I may mention that, before I took my degree,
he wished to know what books I was reading with a
view to it. On my mentioning the names of a few
books indirectly bearing on the examination, he cut

me short with the paradoxical advice : ' You had better read Shakespeare instead !' On another occasion he quoted to me a remark of the late Poet Laureate, tending to show that that high authority considered Shakespeare to be a writer wholly *sui generis.* 'Tennyson,' he said in effect, ' once told me that he could form an idea of the intellectual efforts of such poets as Byron and Shelley; he did not say that he could have written as well as they did, but their state of mind and feeling was comprehensible to him. But of the state of mind and feeling which found expression in Shakespeare's plays he could form no conception whatever.'*

Being, therefore, an appreciator of art, Jowett must have weighed his words before alleging that ' Art is the bloom of decay.' Is the allegation wholly or partially correct? It cannot be wholly correct ; for the poetry of Homer must have been the ' bloom ' of early spring. I am tempted to add that the manifold and unrivalled achievements of the age of Pericles were the bloom of midsummer. But I express this opinion with some hesitation, for Professor Hort seems to have been quoting the view of some high authorities when he once said to me that Greece was declining at the close of the Persian War,

* As Tennyson regarded the inspiration of Shakespeare as incomprehensible even to himself, so he regarded the inspiration of poets in general as incomprehensible, except to poets. At Jowett's table I met the late Professor Lushington, Tennyson's brother-in-law, whose marriage has been immortalized in ' In Memoriam.' He told me that Tennyson used to say : ' People in general have no notion of the way in which we poets go to work.'

and that the glory of Athens was merely a superb 'autumnal glow.' Mill, perhaps, owing to his political bias, took an opposite view. He abhorred the fatalistic dilettantism which loves to affirm or imply that the sound and vigorous part of national life must be over before the artistic part can begin ; insomuch that a nation, after the manner of a caterpillar, has to lay up a store of energy during a period of long and sordid obscurity, merely that it may have a brief space of ineffectual beauty at the close. In short, Mill, with his zeal for Liberty, regarded her as the mother of all excellence, artistic excellence included. The masterpieces of the Augustan age present an obvious objection to such a view, and it may be worth while to quote the passage in which he deals with that objection :

'The despotism of the Cæsars fostered many of the graces of life, and intellectual cultivation in all departments not political ; it produced monuments of literary genius dazzling to the imaginations of shallow readers of history, who do not reflect that the men to whom the despotism of Augustus (as well as of Lorenzo de Medici and of Louis XIV.) owes its brilliancy were all formed in the generation preceding. The accumulated riches, and the mental energy and activity, produced by centuries of freedom, remained for the benefit of the first generation of slaves.'

The last sentence would be intelligible enough if Mill had merely meant that the first generation of slaves could enjoy what the generations of freedom had produced ; but the odd thing is that the generation of slaves produced what the generation of freemen could not produce. So, again, Mill would have triumphed over the 'shallow readers of history' if the political and the literary history of Rome had been like the bars of a parallel ruler when those bars are a little apart, so that the one bar is somewhat in advance of the other; that is to say, if the birth, maturity and decay of Roman freedom had respectively preceded by a quarter of a century the birth, maturity and decay of the great Roman literature. But this was notoriously not the case. The republic was in a far sounder condition during the Second Punic War than during the Civil War between Marius and Sylla. Why, then, did Roman literature burst into 'bloom' shortly after the Civil War and the proscriptions, and not shortly after the defeat of Hannibal?

It is, therefore, hard to doubt that, as there is what may be called a literature of maturity, so there is also a kind of literature which seldom springs up save in times of decadence. Also, this literature of decadence is gaining in popularity. Sometimes, no doubt, we are fascinated by the buoyant and combative vigour which animates such early poems as those of Homer, and as the song of Deborah and Barak. This fascination springs from a sense of extreme contrast. But a fascination of this sort operates by fits and starts, and belongs exclusively to poetry of the highest order. In general, the contrast, to be lastingly effectual, must be less extreme. We like to be able, without any troublesome effort, to enter into the spirit of what we read. Therefore, poetry modern in spirit has a special fitness for us. And, as poetry (like population) multiplies, the great principle of the survival of the fittest, and of the elimination of the less fit, must or should be brought to bear upon it. Thus it is that when we have to make our choice from the poems of a nation alien to us in language, in social institutions and religion, we naturally give the preference to the poems which were written in an advanced state of civilization, which remind us (though with a difference) of our own introspective and melancholy musings, and which emphatically are *the bloom of decay*. I am often quoting Scherer in this Memoir, because he had something in common both with Pattison and with Jowett; for he had combined the former's philosophical scepticism with the latter's unwavering adhesion to high ethical ideals. In the present instance I will quote a passage in which he is himself repeating with assent an opinion of Renan :

' On a calomnié, selon lui [Renan] les périodes de décadence ; les civilisations vieillies sont les civilisations exquises, et les littératures doivent leurs fleurs les plus brillantes à la fermentation des sociétés qui se décomposent.'

It may be worth while to refer to another speculation of Renan—a speculation which indirectly throws light on Jowett's half-unconscious doubts about progress. Renan expected that the day will come when French ideas will overflow all the world ; but with this expectation he coupled the foreboding that, when the mission of France is thus fulfilled, France herself may be no more. But can we be quite sure, he might also have asked, that the world, when thus

fertilized by French thought, will always continue to
bear fruit? Will not the summer be succeeded by
winter? Or will not the world-wide soil at last be
exhausted? Speculations like those of Jowett may
lead some of his disciples—as Pearson was led—to
entertain, at least in moments of depression, such
doubts as are here indicated. *Debemur morti nos
nostraque.* Civilization may, after all, be nought but
a colossal soap-bubble. When it seems to have
reached perfection in volume and in symmetry, in
beauty and in mobility, it may be on the point of
bursting.

Before concluding my estimate of Jowett's attitude towards the cause of Liberalism and progress,
I will quote two random remarks of his which make
for Liberalism. First, he said that Italy seemed to
him to owe more to the party of Mazzini than is
generally acknowledged. And, secondly, on its being
hinted that Conservatives complain of being assailed
with the weapons of rhetoric and ridicule, he insisted
that, from the time of Aristophanes to that of the
Anti-Jacobin, quite as much satirical wit has been
employed on the Conservative side as on the side of
Revolution.

I spoke of Jowett's doubts about progress as 'half
unconscious.' It may be well to offer a few examples
of his propensity to envelop himself in an intellectual haze, and, in a word, of his dislike to being
catechized, and even to catechize himself. He
objected to lying even in extreme cases. He told
me that he had a friend of the highest sense of

honour who was often entrusted with important secrets. Questions in regard to those secrets were sometimes put to him which were of such a nature that, if he refused to answer them, he would have revealed the secrets. In those circumstances he did what most of us would have done—*he kept faith by lying*. 'I will not say that this was wrong,' said Jowett, 'but I don't think that it was quite right.' On another occasion, a friend—surely a descendant of Boswell—put a case to him : 'Imagine that you saw a weak man running away in terror of his life, and that presently a strong man came with a drawn sword, and asked if you had seen the weak man, would you not answer "No"?'

J.—'No doubt anyone would in such a case. But I don't see any use in imagining such cases before they arise.'

It seems to have been a set principle with Jowett that persons who have recourse to what he once called 'exceptional morality' ought to keep the matter to themselves. In 'Safe Studies,' p. 265, I speak of an Oxford don who was nicknamed 'Presence of Mind,' in consequence of a story told by himself. 'A friend,' he used to relate, 'invited me to go out with him on the water. The sky was threatening, and I declined. At length he succeeded in persuading me, and we embarked. A squall came on, the boat lurched, and my friend fell overboard. Twice he sank, and twice he rose to the surface. He placed his hands on the prow and endeavoured to climb in. There was great apprehension lest he should upset the boat. Providentially I had brought my umbrella with me. I had the presence of mind to strike him two or three hard blows over the knuckles. He let go his hold and sank. The boat righted itself, and we were saved.' On hearing of this incident, Jowett said : ' I don't say that he was wrong ; but he deserved to be called "Presence of Mind" for talking about it as he did.' In taking this apologetic tone, Jowett doubtless meant to imply that the not over-zealous friend might have contended that it was expedient that one man rather than that the whole party should perish. When thus stated, the principle is not easily impugned ; but, if it is once admitted, it has an obvious application to the terrible remedy to which sailors have sometimes had recourse under pressure of famine.

I heard him, in a lecture on the ' Republic,' refer to the famous question raised by Glaucon : Suppose that a man, by committing enormous crimes, obtained great power and prosperity, and that he was secure of impunity in the next world as well as in this. Why should we not prefer his lot to that of a just man who fares ill ?

J.—' He might have gone a step further, and supposed that the unjust man had a good conscience and the just man a bad one. The fact is that nobody has any business to put such cases. We cannot conceive of virtue and vice apart from their natural accompaniments.'*

* Ethical puzzles repeat themselves. In the schoolboy's query : ' Would you rather be a bigger fool than you look, or

Two short sayings of Jowett's may show how he skirted the labyrinth of life's problems, or, rather, how he turned some of those problems (as Goethe recommended) into postulates. I repeated to him the old commonplace that wealth does not bring happiness. Jowett replied that this was nonsense: 'All men seek wealth, and in doing so they assume it to be a good.' On another occasion, I contended that increase of knowledge is increase of sorrow.

J.—'No; you should take Aristotle's view that the acquisition of knowledge is in itself an aim.'

The following curious passage from Gibbon's 'Memoirs' would have obtained Jowett's warm approval: 'M. d'Alembert relates that, as he was walking in the gardens of Sans Souci with the King of Prussia, Frederick said to him: " Do you see that old woman, a poor weeder, asleep on that sunny bank? She is probably a more happy being than either of us." The King and the philosopher may speak for themselves; for my part, I do not envy the old woman.'

The remark made by Jowett about humour, which I quoted above, reminds me that the question is sometimes asked: Had Jowett much sense of humour? In the hope of throwing light on this subject, I will quote from a letter written to me

---

look a bigger fool than you are?' for 'fool' read 'rogue,' and understand 'look' to mean 'permanently look'; and you have before you a moral riddle almost, if not quite, identical with that which the Greek sophists put, and which Glaucon failed to answer.

by a friend. 'Jowett mentioned that Hawkins, in his "Life," described Dr. Johnson as the most humorous man he had ever known. The Master went on to say that one could hardly gather that impression from Boswell, adding that he thought Boswell, being a Scotchman, had missed the humour of Johnson.'* Is it possible that Jowett, in passing this judgment, failed to observe in what diverse senses the word *humour* is employed? He himself undoubtedly relished a kind of humour; he enjoyed the humour of Plato. I was staying with him at Freshwater when he read 'Silas Marner' for the first time, and I noticed how he enjoyed the humouristic touches that it contains. On the whole, his humour seems to have resembled the humour of Addison; it had little in common with the humour of Montaigne, of Swift, or of Sterne.†

---

* Jowett, however, was a great admirer and a constant reader of the 'Life of Johnson.' I once heard him exclaim: 'L—— C—— says that if he were thrown on a desert island he would like to have the Bible, Plato, and Shakespeare. I should be disposed to add Boswell.'

† It is remarkable that such a serious writer as Edmond Scherer felt sympathy with the typical humorist after the fashion of Sterne, who well knows that the human lot is mean and pitiful, but who 'prend doucement son parti, et s'en amuse plutôt qu'il s'en scandalise.' Elsewhere he says: 'Le monde est surtout un spectacle, un spectacle dans lequel les agitations de l'esprit, les obscurités des problèmes, les conceptions idéales, dans lequel les vains efforts de l'humanité, dans lequel la vertu même aux prises avec le mal, font partie du programme, et contribuent à l'intérêt de la représentation.' Pattison would have echoed this sentiment, Jowett would not. Still less would the two men have agreed with Jules Lemaître, who somewhere says: 'Si Dieu a fait le songe de tous et sait ce qu'il a fait, il doit se divertir prodigieusement.'

He would not have liked Montaigne's statement that our human nature deserves all the ridicule that can be cast upon it ('est autant ridicule que risible'). I once quoted to him Horace Walpole's famous saying that 'This world is a comedy to those who think, a tragedy to those who feel'; and he surprised me by not being familiar with the aphorism, and seemingly not being struck by it. Still less would he have sympathized with Lord Houghton, who writes somewhat broadly:

'The contrasts, the inconsistencies, the incongruities, which provoke and exercise the faculty of humour are really invisible to most persons, or, when perceived, arouse a totally distinct order of ideas and associations. It must seem to them at best a mischievous inclination to find a source of mirth in the sufferings and struggles, and troubles of others; and when the humorist extends this practice to himself, and discovers a certain satisfaction in his own weaknesses and miseries, introverting the very sensations of pleasure and pain, he not only checks the sympathy he might otherwise have won, but his very courage is interpreted into an unnatural audacity, alike defiant of the will of Heaven and of the aid of man. The deep consolations of this faculty in the trials and extremities of life are altogether unknown to them.'

In fact, he might have said of history in general what Fitzgerald, the poet, said of the great work of Tacitus—it is 'full of pleasant atrocities'—*quibus ipse malis careas quia cernere suave est.*

On the whole, therefore, Jowett had little or no world-humour. He took things too seriously to derive entertainment from the all-pervading discrepancy between the ideal and the actual—between the world of aspiration and the world of fact. He could play with the small anomalies, but not with the great anomaly, of life. Not, indeed, that he was wholly insensible to the humorous side of tragic events. When the Chinese put down the Taeping rebellion with Oriental ferocity, it was said that a number of captive rebels were made to stand in a row with their necks on the same level, so that the executioner could behead them with a single sweep of his sword. Jowett mentioned this singular economy of time, as we may call it, to a party of us who were dining with him at Balliol; and, by way of giving effect to the narration, he ran down the Common Room with outstretched arm in jocular imitation of the headsman. If it be thought that in so doing he laid aside his wonted gravity, it should be remembered that a Chinaman was then (if he is not still) regarded as a sort of joke, and that his exclusive and disdainful country lay, as it were, beyond the confines of the philanthropist's map. The foregoing incident, therefore, seems to me less surprising than that which I am about to relate, though it may prepare the way for it. A shy student, chancing to sit next Jowett at dinner, and being at a loss for a topic of conversation, stumbled on the unpromising one of murder. To his surprise, the Master rose to the bait, mentioned some *causes célèbres*, and dropped all formality. The you Oxonian afterwards asked a friend who knew Jo better than he himself did whether he had ever a similar experience with the Master. 'If you get Jowett to talk about murders,' replied the friend (in effect), 'he will go off like a house on fire.' This singular predilection can hardly have been due to a mere love of sensational excitement;* the true explanation probably is that, as a psychologist, he wished to explore the darkest abysses of human nature; and perhaps, too, he could better afford to take an outside and dispassionate view of that most heinous of crimes than of some more venial sins, because the crime was one which it was morally impossible that he, or those with whom he discussed it, would ever be tempted to commit. He would have forborne to enlarge on that diverting topic if he had been speaking to a criminal under capital sentence.

Jowett told a story that a young Oriental (I think a prince), after studying at Oxford, was so unfortunate when he returned to his native land as to have contracted the habit of intoxication; that the elders of his country, pointing at him the finger of scorn, used significantly to exclaim, ' Oxford!' and that in consequence the national wits came to employ sometimes the name of Oxford and sometimes its initial

---

* Macaulay was told by a Killarney boatman that the pleasure which he had derived twenty years before from rowing Sir Walter Scott and Miss Edgeworth on the lake, had made amends to him for having missed seeing a man hanged on that day. Might not a modern Rochefoucauld contend that the gratification which this boatman derived from witnessing executions, and which not a few educated men derive from hearing and talking of murders, is in each instance largely composed of the half-consciousness of being so much better off than the murdered man, and so much better off and better than the murderer?

letter to denote the eminently European vice over which that seat of learning, falsely so called, was thought to have cast the spell of her mysterious and meretricious fascination¹* The Master once told me of an orthodox divine who maintained that unbaptized persons have no souls. Hence it would follow that Baptists who die in early youth will have no future life. ' But this,' continued Jowett, ' would be letting Dissenters off too cheap. So he added that God miraculously implants souls in them, in order to damn them eternally.'

Of course Jowett had the strongest objection to the coarse humour which is too often found in such writers as Rabelais. His aversion to everything approaching to coarseness is indicated in the often-quoted story that he asked an undergraduate what motto is written over the gate of hell. The under-graduate suggested some motto to the effect that there is no escape (perhaps the motto *Vestigia nulla retrorsum*). ' No,' replied the Master, ' the inscription is, *Ici on parle français.*' I am bound, however, to add that, when he spoke to me of the French, his language was more or less sympathetic. He admitted, indeed, that the relations between husbands and wives in France were often most unsatisfactory, and

---

* As a set-off against this tragic result of the somewhat explosive contact of Eastern with Western civilization, I will subjoin a comic result of that contact. Sir James Fitzjames Stephen used to say that he bought some curious little idols at Benares, and ordered them to be sent to his address at Cal cutta. On their arrival he found that the box containing them was labelled with the delicious inscription, ' Gods with care.' This anecdote, with all that it suggests, would have delighted Jowett, as it evidently delighted Sir James.

he added that they had been so even in the time of
Shakespeare: but he thought, on the other hand,
that the relation between fathers and sons was
pleasanter in that country than in England.

A characteristic incident, related to me by two
eye-witnesses, shows how strongly Jowett felt that
a decorous reticence should be observed in the
presence, not merely of boys, but of young men
(*debetur juveni reverentia*). A distinguished man
who had spent some time in the East, and had
become in a manner denaturalized, dined with
Jowett; and a party of Oxonians, including some
undergraduates, was asked to meet him. The
Orientalized veteran, after the ladies had left the
room, told some anecdotes about Eastern customs,
the narration of which in the presence of young
men was far from edifying. One anecdote, in particular, threatened to be more startling than its
predecessors. There was a general wish to check
the unconscious transgressor, but there was a no
less general unwillingness to say anything which
might hurt his feelings. At last Jowett, after giving
the signal to rise from the table, said to him: ' Shall
we continue the conversation when we have joined
the ladies?' Could any better example be given
either of Jowett's peculiar irony or of his tact?

One or two examples may be subjoined of the sort
of advice which Jowett sometimes gave, and which
obtained for him the credit or discredit of worldly
wisdom. I once received from him the following
counsel: ' Never listen to a man when he abuses his

relations. He will make it up with them, and then
he will hate you for knowing that he abused them.'
On another occasion he said to me : ' A friend of mine
of great practical ability told me that he has laid
down for himself three rules of conduct. *Never
retract. Never explain.** *Get it done and let them
howl.*' Jowett repeated these paradoxical maxims
with a characteristic laugh, which seemed at any
rate not to mark disapproval.

The following example may be given in illustration, not so much of Jowett's humour, as of his
ready wit. I asked him (in 1861) what he thought
of the conduct of the then Bishop of Durham, who
had appointed a highly creditable son-in-law to one
of the best livings in the diocese. ' He is not *worse
than an infidel*,' was the prompt reply.†

In illustration of Jowett's appreciation of wit, I
may mention that Jowett told a friend that he
ranked Sydney Smith next to Swift among English
wits, and added: ' I think Voltaire was more witty
than Swift, and after Voltaire among French writers
possibly Talleyrand.'

After touching on the nature and limitations of
Jowett's humour, and, above all, on his deficiency in
world-humour, we are brought to the question : Had
he always a deep sense of sin? or, Was he ever
afflicted with that relaxation of the moral fibre,
that *affaiblissement de l'idéal*, which Scherer declares

* Goethe says, as nearly as I can remember: ' I hate all
explanations. They often deceive those to whom they are
addressed, and often also those who give them.'
† See 1 Tim. v. 8.

to be the outcome of humour? To prepare the way
for this inquiry, let us first ask, Was he an ethical
reformer? Some of his utterances would suggest a
negative answer to this question. Thus, in the
essay on 'Casuistry,' he writes :

'Numberless questions . . . relating to the professions of
an advocate, a soldier, or a clergyman, have been pursued into
endless consequences. In all these cases there is a point at
which necessity comes in and compels us to adopt the rule of
the Apostle, which may be paraphrased, "Do as other men do
in a Christian country."'

I once quoted the foregoing passage to that ardent
world-betterer, T. H. Green ; he told me that he was
aware that Jowett had laid down this principle, but
that he himself thought it most immoral. And, no
doubt, he was right in thinking that the principle
may be pressed to very odd conclusions. The only
question is whether any other ethical principle can
be laid down which may not be pressed to equally
odd conclusions. Be this as it may, Jowett, when he
counselled acquiescence in conventional morality, was
adopting the tone which is commonly found in Horace.
But he often faced about, as Horace sometimes did,
and became a moralist of the first water ('Virtutis
veræ custos rigidusque satelles '). I think it was
in 1861 that I told Jowett the substance of an article
in the *Saturday Review* on 'Prigs.' The ingenious
essayist, if I remember rightly, used words to the
following effect: 'Suppose an undergraduate who
never scamped his work, and was never once late
either for lecture or for chapel. Would not his neigh-

bours extol his exemplary behaviour? Far from it. They would set him down as an irretrievable prig.' Jowett listened to me with some impatience, and then said: ' Why does the *Saturday Review* always laugh at people who try to be a little better than the rest of the world?' On another occasion he acknowledged that the University Commission had been needlessly vexatious in their dealings with All Souls', whereupon one of his hearers suggested that it seemed 'natural' that the fellows should take the law into their own hands, and that they should now and then elect (as they were reported to have done) a new member into their gentlemanlike Club in blissful disregard of his place in the examination. ' If this is natural,' said Jowett, with some asperity, ' it means that human nature is very bad.' Pattison would doubtless have been disposed to challenge this severe verdict on the ground that human nature furnishes the only standard by which human nature can be judged ; that, therefore, when Jowett broadly declared that human nature is very bad, he showed that he had been expecting from the human animal a greater degree of perfection than appertains to the constitution of that animal; and that, in fact, he spoke as unscientifically as if he had said that most men are very shortlived, or that most men are very small.

Another question bearing on that of the heinousness of sin is the question of Philosophical Necessity. One of the ' stodgy questions' which, as an undergraduate, I put to Jowett was whether he believed in Necessity or in Free Will.

J.—' I believe in Necessity in the sense of believing that our actions are determined by motives.'

T.—' That admission seems to me to cover the entire ground. But would it do to act on the belief ?'

J. [laughing].—' If you begin to act on the belief, we shall have to turn you out of the College. [More seriously] No. Whatever one may think about the abstract question, one does not mean that it is the same thing to be walking along the street of one's free will and to be dragged along it against one's will. Necessity, when rightly understood, remains a sort of theory in the background, and one acts in much the same way whether one believes in it or not.'

Is this exactly so ? Does the belief in Necessity, when held by a thoughtful person, lie dormant in his moral constitution ? Mr. John Morley, indeed, seems to think that this theory need have no very great, or at least no very enervating, effect upon conduct. This appears from the whole passage, in which he says of James Mill :

' Perhaps even at the last he had glimpses of the mood imputed in the saying of divers strong men on their death-beds, from the Emperor Augustus to Rabelais : " *Draw the curtain, the play is over.*" We shall never know how much brave and honest work has been done for the world by men in whose minds lurked all the while this thought of the puppet-show, the tragi-comedy of phantoms.'

Personally, I should have thought that this mood of mind generally makes men rather tolerant than brave. It seems, as a rule, to clip the wings of aspiration. It almost always blunts the edge of righteous anger. If all the world's a show, and all the men and women merely puppets, how can we be wroth with the clumsy and fragile puppets which

'Nature's journeymen' have made? The Philistine moralist feels disgust, and nothing but disgust, at the crimes of Cæsar Borgia. But an anthropologist finds that his disgust is largely tempered with pity when he considers how evil a disposition would probably, and how evil an education would certainly, have fallen to the lot of any son of Alexander VI.—

θεοῖς γὰρ ἦν οὕτω φίλον
τάχ' ἄν τι μηνίουσιν εἰς γένος πάλαι.*

And, in general, such a philosopher will be convinced that those three modern Parcæ—Heredity, Education, and Afterlot—have woven a spell for each one of us and have fashioned us after their liking. When once he has satisfied himself that *L'homme obéit à son tempérament aussi fatalement que l'animal obéit à son instinct,* he will conclude that *Tout comprendre, c'est tout pardonner;* insomuch that perchance, in paradoxical moments, he would be tempted to adapt the familiar couplet, and to exclaim:

' If rogues, like earthquakes, come by Fate's design,
   Why blame a Borgia or a Catiline ?'

But at this point he will find himself in a difficulty. He soon learns that if he is writing a biography, and above all, if he is delivering a popular lecture, his sense of pity for evil-doers, and, perhaps, of entertainment at the oddity of the world—'his thought of the puppet-show'—must be studiously ignored.

* Thus it pleased the gods, angered perchance by the generations of old.

He must preach the exceeding sinfulness of sin, even though he be at times haunted by the thought that the head and front of the sinner's offending may be that he did not manage to have better grandfathers! Perhaps, after all, our philosophical sceptic might sum up his teaching by saying: Human nature is not really bad, but it is only by telling men that it *is* bad that we can hope to make it better.*

Such a philosophical sceptic was Pattison. Jowett seems to me to have held tentatively and half consciously nearly the same opinion which Pattison held deliberately and thoroughly. It may, therefore, be worth while to illustrate Pattison's view somewhat further. He was, perhaps, the most paradoxical man I ever met, and, if he had adopted and adapted what Matthew Arnold calls the harsh and unedifying metaphor of St. Paul, he might have applied that

* Without greater exaggeration than is permissible in an epigram, we may say : ' No man who is not penetrated with the thought of the puppet-show can be a sage ; no man who is so penetrated can be a saint.' This thought of the puppet-show—of the subjection of all phenomena, moral as well as physical, to unchanging laws—is well expressed in the fine stanza of Omar Khayyam :

' With Earth's first Clay.They did the Last Man knead,
And there of the Last Harvest sow'd the Seed :
And the first Morning of Creation wrote
What the Last Dawn of Reckoning shall read.'

I think it was Wendell Holmes who said that many a man dies of a disease the seeds of which were sown a century before he was born. It is at least equally true that many a crime is the outcome of a hereditary taint which manifested itself before the criminal was born. Might not the fate of Anne Boleyn and of Sir Thomas More have been different if Henry VIII. had not been the grandson of Edward IV. and the great-nephew of Richard III. ?

metaphor as follows: 'The Great Potter cannot complain of the defects of the vivacious and loquacious pots which He has shapen amiss. But the welfare of the whole pottery requires that the vigorous pots which are made unto honour, instead of pitying the poor pots which are made unto dishonour, should conspire to chide them for their uncomeliness, and, if need be, to break them in pieces.' That this presentment of his view is not overdrawn may be easily shown. A kinswoman of his informs me that when very young she was perplexed by a saying of his, which seemed to be at variance with the teaching of the Church Catechism. 'There is no such thing,' he told her, 'as sin; there are only mistakes.' From so astounding a proposition Jowett would certainly have recoiled. And yet I persist in thinking that his standpoint and Pattison's were in close vicinity. If called upon to explain himself, Pattison might well have contended that he meant no more than Goethe had meant when he said that 'the man of action is always without a conscience.' He might have gone further, and maintained that his disquieting and unpriestly paradox, when furbished up and made presentable, merely signifies that our moral sentiments and traditions will not bear strict analysis. I have not the smallest doubt that he, if pressed by logic, would have expanded his principle after this manner: 'There is no such thing as sin; there are only mistakes. *But the most fatal of all mistakes would be to desist from speaking and acting as if there were such*

a thing as sin.'   Thus I am confirmed in the opinion
which I expressed ten years ago, namely, that Pattison's ethical creed was 'Utilitarianism tempered by
Pyrrhonism' ('Stones of Stumbling,' p. 167).

To return to Jowett.   The paradox, if paradox it
be, that our moral sentiments become pulverized
under logical pressure, was upheld in my presence by
two of his most distinguished disciples, Henry Smith
and Bowen.   One remark of Bowen's may be worth
quoting as illustrating the Jowettian standpoint.
When I was coaching with him, he said to me :
'If you had talked to Aristotle about the corruption
of human nature, he would have laughed at you.'
Indeed, Jowett himself sometimes pitched his note
in a key not wholly dissimilar.   In one of the essays
that I read to him, I spoke of Socrates as having had
a deep sense of sin.   He cut me short with the
remark that the conception of the heinousness of
sin is not Greek, but Oriental.   In speaking thus, he
seemed to endorse the saying of Carlyle that 'Socrates
is terribly at ease in Zion.'   But he seemed to imply
more than this.   He seemed to intimate that the
belief in the heinousness of sin belongs rather to
the theologian than to the philosopher, and that,
in the philosopher's opinion, at least, this belief
is *man-made* and not *God-made*—is artificial, if not
illusory.   Roughly, then, we may thus distinguish
between Jowett's standpoint and Pattison's.   As a
philosopher, Jowett did not believe in the heinousness of sin; but as a moralist, he did believe in it.
Pattison, as a philosopher, did not believe in it; as

a moralist, he pretended to believe in it, or at most he now and then made himself half believe that he believed in it. The philosopher and the moralist in him were in a manner harnessed together by logic; so that he could not, as Jowett could, let his two selves go careering about in opposite directions. On the whole, therefore, we may conclude that to a logical disciple of Jowett's, as well as to any disciple of Pattison, the sense of sin has a ghostly impressiveness, and, indeed, has much in common. with the representation of a ghost on the stage—he distinctly sees it, but also *he sees through it.* Or perhaps a better illustration would be that to such a one this sense of sin, this imperious Postulate of the Practical Reason, is like the black cap of a Judge—a something external and repulsive which he has to assume when about to pronounce a sentence of the utmost severity, but which he then promptly lays aside. Might not Pattison, or might not Renan, have said of this belief in the heinousness of sin, as Renan has said of another great theological postulate, that its interest lies in the twofold fact that it involves a physical impossibility, and that it is itself a moral necessity?*

* It occurs to me that a moralist, or at least a statesman or a judge, considers his fellow-men as somewhat resembling the pieces on a draught-board; he regards them, for some purposes, as possessing equal capacities, and as therefore giving rise to equal expectations. The philosopher, on the other hand, regards them as resembling chessmen; for he never forgets that different individuals differ widely in capacity, and that very much more is to be expected from some than from others. So considered, the worst knaves of all, the ἀκόλαστοι, the morally blind, may be compared to the knights of chess—they are continually being moved in a crooked course, but they are themselves as unaware that the course is crooked as that there is a Power outside themselves that moves them.

Mill has coupled together Plato and Luther, alleging that each of those great men belonged to the class of intellectual reformers who, having succeeded beyond all reasonable expectation, spend their old age in moderating the ardour of disciples who are eager to outrun their master. In what sense, and on what evidence, this is said of Plato I am curious to learn; but the remark may with much truth be applied to our Oxford Plato. For in his later years, and, indeed, in middle life, Jowett was apprehensive lest some of his pupils should go too far. He was alarmed by the scepticism which he saw spreading among some of the ablest men of my standing at Oxford. He could not imagine, he once said to me, how and where this scepticism was picked up; he was careful not to instil it, but it seemed somehow to arise of itself. He also expressed regret that so few of the most thoughtful men were willing to take orders; the evil had been more or less apparent for some time, but when he spoke to me (about 1859) it was worse than ever. I once read to him an essay which contained some unguarded expressions. When I had done, he said (after a few friendly comments) that I seemed to him to be ridiculing the belief in a future life. I assured him that he had misunderstood me; but he went on to say that a lady friend (Dean Stanley's mother) had told him that she had heard that I was becoming wild in my opinions. He added that he trembled for me when he thought how I was separating myself from the beliefs of those around me. Reflecting in later life on this remark of his, I have sometimes thought it very curious. Aristotle, in a quaintly modern passage, has reprobated the notion that the dead are in no way affected by the fortunes of the living, not as being logically untenable, but as being ‘too heartless and opposed to current opinions’ (λίαν ἄφιλον καὶ ταῖς δόξαις ἐναντίον). And it seems to me to have been in a spirit not wholly unlike this that Jowett eschewed religious scepticism, not as being unsound, or (to use my father's phrase) ‘most displeasing to Almighty God,’ but as involving the sense of loneliness and the paralysis of moral effort, which are the common accompaniments of intellectual isolation. In this instance Jowett, like Pattison, though less consciously and completely, ‘subordinated religion to morality.’

In recording these instances, I specially wish to call attention to Jowett's gentle and sympathetic handling of honest doubt. They present a strong contrast to at least one harsh saying ascribed to him. My readers may remember the story of the somewhat priggish youth who told Jowett that he could not convince himself of the existence of God : ‘I cannot see any signs of Him in Nature, and when I look into my own heart I fail to find Him there.’ J.—‘You must either find Him by to-morrow morning or leave the College.’ Did Jowett really say this ? It is proverbially hard to prove a negative. But I will venture to suggest that, if the story be true, Jowett had made up his mind as to what manner of man he was dealing with, and thought (justly or unjustly) that the pretentious apostle of negation should be brought to the test of martyrdom.

It should also be borne in mind that Jowett was punctilious in enforcing discipline and in avoiding all cause of offence, when, as Master of Balliol, he was establishing in the College a Liberal government, or, as we may now say, a Liberal dynasty, to supplant the reactionary government which had so long borne sway. Not only is it true that new brooms sweep clean, but also in the cleansing process they are apt to be stiff, prickly, and rough :

Ἅπας δὲ τραχύς, ὅστις ἂν νέον κρατῇ.

And in very truth Jowett *was* a reformer, successful beyond all reasonable expectation. A great statesman once said of Mr. Bright that he was specially fortunate in having, before the close of his life, won the regard of his old enemies. Jowett did less and more than this. He seldom or never won the regard of his old enemies. But he won, not only the regard, but the affection, of their children and grandchildren. He educated the younger generation first to tolerate and then to admire him. And thus it is that now, when some worthy philanthropists and landlords

‘ in dust repose,
Whose sons shall blush their fathers were his foes,’

he has taken high rank among the Whigs of Religion —among those who, Conservatives in the true sense, have averted revolution by making timely concessions.

How, then, did he maintain himself in this midway position? In answering this, I will endeavour to throw light on his manner of dealing with what may be called the Paley-Butler arguments, which drive men to extremes. The main argument of Butler's ' Analogy,' or something very like it, has been used by the narrowly orthodox party against all its opponents except its extreme ones. The Extreme Right in religion employs the weapon against the Right Centre and the Left Centre, but it fails to touch the Extreme Left. Nay, to the Extreme Left —to the atheists—this same weapon is not unacceptable. In a less degree this has now become true of Paley's argument in support of miracles. The argument that, if you accept one miracle, you must be prepared to accept all the miracles which Paley defends ; and that, if you accept these, you must also be prepared to accept all the miracles which Cardinal Newman defends, is assuredly two-edged. In fact, bigots and atheists, though they would, of course, word the argument differently, agree in insisting that ' ce n'est que le premier pas qui coute,' and that the beginning of supernaturalism is as when one letteth out water. It was, I understand, either Charles or Arthur Buller who (so to say) christened Mr. Grote a ' rigid Atheist.' At any rate, Mr. Grote showed the appropriateness of the name by saying to me : ' It is of no use striking at the branches so long as you leave the root. The belief in a God seems to me to be the root and germ of every form of superstition.' And when I praised Jowett to him, he said

9

that Mill had in like manner praised the theological liberalism of Sterling.*   But he himself seemed to have a sort of *timeo Danaos* feeling about Jowett and Sterling alike. 'Les esprits faibles ne sont jamais sincères,' says Rochefoucauld, with much exaggeration. Grote would, I suspect, have regarded both Jowett and Sterling as speculatively *des esprits faibles;* and yet he would have considered them certainly as sincere, and probably as trustworthy, but hardly as in the fullest sense reliable.

How, then, did Jowett avoid both the horns of the dilemma, one of which transfixed Newman, while the other transfixed Grote? A biographer, like a critic, must as far as possible keep himself in the background; so I will seek to trace out Jowett's standpoint without being careful to determine my own. I once called Jowett's attention to Blanco White's extraordinary assertion that no sincere Catholic can be tolerant, and to Buckle's comment on that assertion, that a sincere Catholic may be, and often is, tolerant — a consistent Catholic, never.   Jowett thought that even Buckle's statement is extravagant: 'It involves the whole question whether Catholicism can adapt itself to the needs of the present day.' Now, it is plain that, if the doctrines of the Bible or of the Church are absolutely true, and conflict with the so-called needs of the present day, the needs ought to adapt themselves to the

* Part of this is stated, and more of it is implied, in my Recollections of Grote ('Safe Studies,' p. 141), but during the lifetime of Mrs. Grote I expressed myself guardedly.

doctrines, and not the doctrines to the needs. So, again, I once talked over with him Professor Rawlinson's Bampton Lectures, in which the truth of the Bible was sought to be confirmed by inscriptions and other recent discoveries. Jowett made the characteristic comment on them : ' Everybody admits that there was a king who was called Solomon, and built a temple. What Rawlinson proves is virtually matter of this sort, matter which nobody doubts. But in much that he tries to prove he must fail. *He is trying to pitch the standard of belief too high for the present age.*' Here the highest criticism of the age is made the ultimate Court of Appeal. Jowett took hold of the criticism of the age with strong grappling-irons. He had a more working belief— Newman would have said a more ' *real* belief '—in that criticism than in the teaching of tradition ; if criticism and tradition came into collision, tradition must go to the wall.

And now, in order further to illustrate Jowett's point of view, I will make a last comparison between it and Pattison's. Not long ago, I quoted a suggestion of Mr. Francis Galton to the effect that our poor little planet may be no better than a *lusus Naturæ*, a sort of cosmic malformation. Carrying out this illustration, a disciple of Pattison might ask : ' If our world is a cripple, may not the cripple have need of a crutch ? In other words, may not illusion, that twin-sister of symbolism, be indispensable for morality—indispensable temporarily, and perhaps even permanently?' A disciple of

Jowett would hesitate to take this line; at all events, he would not be so explicit. Perhaps the difference between Pattison and Jowett may be best indicated by saying that Pattison, as we have seen, practised *economy of truth*, whereas Jowett rather practised *economy of logic*.* Jowett did this in an extreme form when he accepted general principles, and refused to follow them out to their conclusions. When he thus conveniently exiled himself from 'the dominion of logic,' he touched the frontier line which divides economy of logic from economy of truth. Sometimes he even seemed to cross that frontier. I remember talking to him about H. N. Oxenham's reputation as a speaker in the Union. Jowett seemed to think his reputation exaggerated, and to regard Oxenham himself as aggressively and tiresomely argumentative. The man who had most impressed Jowett by his power of condensing an argument into

---

* A very singular and plain-spoken passage from Amiel's *Journal Intime* may serve to illustrate my meaning: 'Ce double fait contradictoire, d'une espérance naïve renaissant après toutes les déceptions et d'une expérience presque invariablement défavorable, s'explique comme toutes les illusions par une volonté de la nature, qui veut *que nous soyons abusés ou que nous agissions comme si nous l'étions encore.* Le scepticisme est plus sage, mais il paralyse la vie, en supprimant l'erreur. La maturité d'esprit consiste à entrer dans le jeu obligé en se domant l'air d'être dupe. Cette complaisance débonnaire corrigée par une sourire est encore le parti le plus ingénieux.' The words I have italicized roughly mark the difference between Jowett and Pattison. In times of introspection, Jowett would perhaps have half acknowledged the principle contained in the words 'que nous soyons abusés'; Pattison, at such times, which with him were very frequent, would have quite acknowledged the principle contained in the words 'que nous agissions comme si nous l'étions encore.'

the fewest possible words was Ward. He gave me an instance of this. He said that Ward, while still an Anglican, had spoken to him of the Evangelicals who failed to find the doctrine of baptismal regeneration in the Church Service. 'I do not blame them,' continued Ward, 'for thus using words in a non-natural sense ; *but we are all dishonest together, and therefore we are all honest.*' Jowett seemed to me to quote this epigram with approval. The words, I submit, must mean that all Anglicans are and must be illogical, but they are illogical more or less consciously according to their greater or less degree of culture. A yet more singular utterance of Jowett's tended in the same direction. A distinguished writer, who had been somewhat persecuted for Rationalism's sake, had subsequently made profession of such spotless orthodoxy as to awaken suspicion among his enemies that he was all things to all men, or, rather, to all women. I spoke to Jowett about him, and looked inquiringly. 'The worst of it is that he'll end by believing it all,' replied Jowett, with that enigmatical and (in the Greek sense) *ironical* smile which sometimes made it hard to tell whether our modern Socrates was speaking half in jest or wholly in earnest.

The foregoing examples set forth one side of Jowett, the side which he had in common with Pattison. The next example shows a very different side of him. When I was an undergraduate, I once, having caught the spirit of one of his most advanced pupils, tried to embody that spirit in an essay which

I showed to Jowett himself. In that essay I threw out the suggestion that, if some illusions are indeed beatific and (so to say) bonific, it must be a folly to disillusionize one's self and a crime to disillusionize others, and I concluded with the words: ' Thus scepticism, when carried to the furthest point, destroys itself, and leads us by an indirect path in speculation to orthodoxy, and in practice to a colourless acquiescence in the principles of our own time.' This juvenile outburst, which was meant, I now hope, to draw Jowett out, succeeded in doing so more than I could have expected. I give his comment from memory, but it was, I think, as follows: ' Do you really suppose this to be the whole truth ? I cannot believe it. Even if such scepticism prevails for a time, it must sooner or later pass away.' This reminds me that I once asked him what he thought of that most unbiblical of books, Ecclesiastes, and how he explained the glaring discordance between the concluding section and the rest of it. What view did he take of its author, if, indeed, there was but one author ?

J.—' He was an arrant sceptic, but in the end a better mind came over him.'

It may not be amiss to sum up in a few words the contrast, which I have so often indicated, between Pattison and Jowett. Pattison knew that social martyrdom is the goal to which the principles of Idealists, if logically pressed, would often lead ; and his own belief in posthumous rewards and punishments had faded away. Hence, being such as he was, and not coveting the barren laurels of an *un-heaven-rewarded* martyrdom, he ended by giving up his Idealism. The antipodes of such a character may be represented by the saint who unquestioningly fights the good fight, who knows that his Vindicator liveth, and who, through all tribulations and misconstructions, looks forward to a sanction which is not of this world. Such born saints as are thus animated and sustained, whatever may be their limitations, seek and find in their devotion to the Ideal their own exceeding great reward. *The Lord is unto them an everlasting light, and their God their glory.* But such a born saint Jowett was not; he had not (to speak broadly) the requisite faculty of ready belief. Thus it was that with neither of the two classes of persons whom I have indicated—neither with Montaigne nor with Pascal, neither with Pattison nor with Liddon—was he completely in accord. His heart was the heart of an Idealist, but his head was the head of a Sceptic. Hence it appears that his unique fascination and his incompleteness arose from the same cause: he sought to combine the *pococurantism* of the sage with the *moltocurantism* of the saint.

It is hoped that these various glimpses of Jowett may be combined into a sort of composite photograph, which will give a not wholly incorrect impression of that ever-changing, but ever-fascinating, spiritual figure. In my youth I had a ready answer to the riddle which his personality presented.

I used to say that, half accepting and half rejecting Christianity, he set things right by accepting half Christianity and rejecting the other half. Perhaps, indeed, it may with truth be said that, in his dealings with orthodoxy, he put into action the two French sayings, ' J'en prends et j'en laisse,' and ' J'y suis et j'y reste.' But to say this and no more would be most unjust, as well as most unfriendly. In reality, he was moved by the suggestion that there may be more things in heaven and earth than are dreamt of in our philosophy. But he may, at the same time, have felt—some of his disciples have certainly felt—that it is hard to draw much comfort from this suggestion without doing violence to the imperious and generally accepted Law of Parsimony, which forbids us to multiply existences, or modes of existence, beyond what is necessary— beyond the point which positive evidence warrants. For example : There is not a particle of evidence to disprove the existence of fairies ; but, as there is no evidence to prove their existence, the case goes against them by default. Our mental attitude towards them is one, not of suspended judgment, but of disbelief. Why should not, one sometimes asks in one's own despite, a similar mode of reasoning be applied to the belief in certain other Invisible Beings?

The burden of this difficulty weighed on the sensitive Amiel, whose state of mind may illustrate Jowett's. In the ' Journal Intime ' Amiel asks whether illusions may not be indispensable, and, if so, how are we to deal with them? He replies: 'La méthode serait peut-être de distinguer profondément l'opinion de la croyance et la croyance de la science. Un esprit qui discerne ces divers degrés peut s'imaginer et peut croire, sans être exclus d'un progrès ultérieur.'

Amiel here commends the use of a sort of sliding scale of beliefs, the preference being given to the belief in science as opposed to the belief in tradition. A somewhat similar sliding scale is indicated in a very remarkable passage which Jowett has inserted in his introduction to the 'Phædo':

'We are more certain of the existence of God than we are of the immortality of the soul, and are led by the belief in the one to a belief in the other. . . . Nor need we shrink from pressing the analogy one step further: "We are more certain of our ideas of truth and right than we are of the existence of God, and are led on in the order of thought from one to the other."'

To the three links in the chain—duty, God, immortality—which Jowett has here connected with each other and arranged in this order, one is tempted to add two more links, one at each end. He would have admitted, at all events in his later years, that the belief in the Christian Revelation is dependent on, and is in a sense subordinate to, the belief in immortality. On the other hand, he would perhaps have acknowledged—Pattison and Fitzjames Stephen would undoubtedly have acknowledged—that the belief in mathematical and in some scientific truths carries with it greater certainty than the belief in the grandest postulates of morality; the equality of the angles at the base of an isosceles triangle is more demonstrable than the obligation of self-sacrifice. On the whole, it may safely be affirmed of such a man as Amiel or Jowett that, in the province of tradition, as the French would say, *il glisse;* in the province of science and of criticism, *il s'appuie.* This is so; but it does not follow that Jowett's affections ran parallel with his convictions. Speaking roughly, we may say that his head was on the side of science; but it was not on that account true that (so to express it) where his head was there his heart was also. He thought with the Rationalists, but felt with the Christians. Perhaps it is not too fanciful to say that, being tossed on the sea of doubt and scepticism, and drifting further and further from his old moorings, he was yet attached to those moorings by an indefinitely elastic cable, and by a golden anchor—the elastic cable of the Imagination, and the golden anchor of Hope. Last summer I was in a Swiss mortuary chapel looking at some human skulls which were arranged in a grotesque pattern on the wall; and, standing where I did, I caught sight of a crucifix in an obscure place further off. Presently, as I gazed at this twofold spectacle—the handiwork of Death close to me, and the dim form in the distance—the words seemed to ring in my ears: *I am the Resurrection and the Life. The hour cometh when the dead shall hear the voice of the Son of God; and they that hear shall live.* And then, as the unuttered voice died away, I somehow found myself thinking of Jowett. Was he not, in very truth, made perfect through suffering? At any rate, let us hope that any of his disciples who have gone, or are going, through the like sore trial, may come out of it as scathless as he did:

> 'Tunc me biremis præsidio scaphæ
> Tutum per Ægæos tumultus
> Aura feret.'

Will it be said that to cherish the Wider Hope, without alleging any evidence for that hope, is mere unfaithfulness to truth? Jowett would probably have replied that such evidence is not wholly wanting. Pandora's box is called, and perhaps thought, empty, because it is less full than each of us in early youth expected it to be. But some solid contents it assuredly has, or so volatile an ingredient as Hope would have evaporated. In brief, Jowett might have echoed the reply made by Prévost-Paradol to the Scotch busybody who asked him to what Church he belonged: 'J'appartiens à cette grande Église sans nom, dont les membres sont partout, et partout se reconnaissent où ils se rencontrent.'

Jowett once praised to me the beauty of the Authorized Version of the New Testament, which he regarded as sometimes, especially in the Apocalypse, superior to the Greek original. By way of illustration, he repeated the text: 'And I, John,

saw the holy city, new Jerusalem, coming down
from God out of heaven, prepared as a bride adorned
for her husband.' As he quoted those magnificent
words, his voice betrayed more of saintly emotion
than I ever observed in it before or since. His un-
wonted earnestness made me feel that the New Jerusalem, whatever mystical sense he might put upon
it, was in very deed the symbol and goal of his
aspirations; his religion, like Dr. Arnold's, and also
like Matthew Arnold's, led

> ' On to the city of God.'

But was not this religion of his mobile and, as it
were, undulating? Unquestionably. But we may,
I think, trace out the limits between which it ebbed
and flowed. The low-water mark may be shown in
words borrowed by him from Socrates : ' There can
no evil happen to a good man in life or death.'

On the other hand, the high-water mark of his
religion may be indicated by saying that, like most
religious philosophers of our day, but more than
most of them, he cherished an ennobling aspiration
which, superficially at least, is more Platonic than
Christian. He was one of those happily constituted
persons who keep alive the hope which is born of an
ardent wish, and is its own and its only justification
—the hope that there is an Ideal World in which
Absolute Goodness, of which the highest earthly
goodness is but a feeble and transient reflection,
has its habitation in perfect fulness and for ever.
Felices ter et amplius! And yet, alas! when I think

upon this cheering and elevating faith of his—this hope of posthumous bliss, untainted by the fear of posthumous ill—I cannot but feel how rare such an unadulterated optimism, the only optimism worthy to be so called, has been throughout the ages, and I exclaim with a sigh : *Many prophets and many philosophers have desired to see those things which he saw, and have not seen them, and to believe those things that he believed, and have not believed them.*

THE END.

BILLING AND SONS, PRINTERS, GUILDFORD.

of whom Mr. Tollemache is almost an English counterpart, there is a richer vein of thought and of philosophy running through all this lighter matter.'—*Anglican Church Magazine.*

'Mr. Tollemache's essays seem to us to possess literary merit of a rare and high order. He is not only pleasantly anecdotic ; he is eminently sympathetic, ingenious, thoughtful, and appreciative, and many of these qualities are also exhibited in his more speculative and less personal papers. His recollections of Grote, Charles Austin, and Pattison are full of interesting anecdote and suggestive comment, while those of Babbage, Sir Charles Wheatstone, Dean Stanley, and Canon Kingsley, belong to the same order. We can best enforce our favourable judgment of these remarkable volumes by quoting a passage from a letter received from Pattison, to whom he had sent the privately printed edition, which, of course, did not contain the paper on Pattison himself : " I should say that the papers on the whole show a union, which is very uncommon, of two opposite qualities, viz., a dominant interest in speculation of a wide and human character, with vast resources, in the memory, of single facts, incidents, or *mots* of famous men. How, with your eyesight, you ever compassed such a range of reading as is here brought to bear at all points of your argument must be a matter of wonder. It seems as if you could draw at pleasure upon all literature, from the classics down to Robert Montgomery and Swinburne." In this judgment we cordially concur. It should be added that the larger volume, entitled " Safe Studies," contains a series of graceful poems by Mrs. Tollemache. . . . The " Recollections of Pattison " are very charming.'—*The Times.*

'These very interesting and, in part, very amusing volumes. . . . Altogether, we can give very hearty praise to the book, and that is something in the case of matter which has not the charm of novelty to the reviewer, and with a good deal of which he disagrees in opinion. Mr. Tollemache can tell an excellent story (such as that of the young lady who, having spoken enthusiastically about a clergyman, and being asked if she referred to any sermon of his, said, " No ; oh no ! But he hates *mayonnaise*, and so do I."). He manages, though he himself is very frequently in presence, and the subject of discussion, never to be unpleasantly egotistic. His work has the literary flavour throughout, without being merely bookish, and he can argue a thesis like a craftsman and a master of his craft.'—*Saturday Review.*

'The "Safe Studies" are those to which it is impossible for any human creature to raise the smallest objection on any ground whatever, and they are about four times as long as the "Stones of Stumbling." These stumbling-blocks may possibly at some period or other have given scandal to a part of the population by no means likely to read them ; but in these days the public has swallowed so many camels that we do not think Mr. Tollemache's gnats would even make any considerable portion of them cough. . . . We propose to make some observations on the most important of these charming essays. They are all singularly well worth reading, and may be described as the works of a most ingenious, accomplished, and cultivated man of leisure, who writes in order to fix recollections and systematize speculations which interest him, and not for the purpose of advocating particular views in the spirit of a partizan or propagandist. . . . The only likelihood of Charles Austin being remembered at all lies in the chance of the survival of the touching and striking account given of him by his accomplished, grateful, and most appreciative pupil.'—*The late Mr. Justice Fitzjames Stephen in the* ST. JAMES'S GAZETTE.

LONDON : WILLIAM RICE, 86, FLEET STREET, E.C.

Mr. EDWARD ARNOLD'S

LIST OF

NEW AND FORTHCOMING WORKS,

October, 1895.

NOTICE.—Mr. Edward Arnold has now opened an Office at 70, Fifth Avenue, New York, from which all his new Books are distributed in America.

THE LAND OF THE NILE SPRINGS.

By COLONEL SIR HENRY COLVILE, K.C.M.G., C.B., recently British Commissioner in Uganda.

With Photogravure Frontispiece, 16 Full-page Illustrations and 2 Maps, demy 8vo., 16s.

SUMMARY OF CONTENTS.—The Road to the Lake—Usoga Uganda—Kampala—Preparations for War—Concentration on the Frontier—Crossing the Kafu—Occupation of the Capital—Chasing Kabarega—The Investment of the Forest—Occupation of Kibiro—The Magungu Expedition—The Wadelai Expedition—The Chain of Forts—Return to Uganda—Parade and Policy—Life at Port Alice—Affairs at Unyoro, etc.

LONDON:
EDWARD ARNOLD, 37 BEDFORD STREET, STRAND.

FIRE AND SWORD IN THE SUDAN.

A personal Narrative of Fighting and Serving the Dervishes, 1879-1895.

By SLATIN PASHA, Colonel in the Egyptian Army, formerly Governor and Commandant of the Troops in Darfur.

Translated and Edited by Major F. R. WINGATE, R.A., D.S.O., *Author of 'Mahdiism and the Egyptian Soudan,' etc.*

Fully Illustrated by R. TALBOT KELLY.

Demy 8vo., One Guinea net.

Slatin Pasha was by far the most important of the European prisoners in the Soudan. Before the Mahdi's victories he held the post of Governor of Darfur, and was in command of large military forces. He fought no fewer than twenty-seven pitched battles before he was compelled to surrender, and is the only surviving soldier who has given an eye-witness account of the terrible fighting that occurred during the Mahdist struggle for supremacy. He was present as a prisoner during the siege of Khartoum, and it was to his feet that Gordon's head was brought in revengeful triumph within an hour of the city's fall.

The narrative is brought up to the present year, when Slatin Pasha's marvellous escape took place, and the incidents of his captivity have been so indelibly graven on his memory that his account of them has all the freshness of a romance.

From a military and historical standpoint the book is of the highest value. Slatin Pasha's various expeditions penetrated into regions as yet almost unknown to Europeans, but destined apparently to be the subject of serious complications in the near future. The map of these regions is believed to be the first authentic one produced. There is also a careful ground-plan of Khartoum and Omdurman, which might be of immense service in case of military operations.

The work is furnished with numerous spirited illustrations by Mr. R. Talbot Kelly, who is personally familiar with the Nile Valley, and has worked under the direct supervision of Slatin Pasha and Major Wingate.

THE ROMANCE OF PRINCE EUGENE.

An Idyll under Napoleon the First.

By ALBERT PULITZER.

With numerous Photogravure Illustrations, in two volumes, demy 8vo., 21s.

EXTRACT FROM THE PREFACE: 'By chance, glancing over the Memoirs and Correspondence of Prince Eugene, published, about forty years ago, by A. du Casse, in ten volumes octavo, I read with real pleasure the letters addressed by the prince to his wife, born Princess-Royal of Bavaria, and considered one of the handsomest women of her time. These letters, written during the stirring transformations of the Napoleonic epoch, reveal, in the exquisite tenderness which they breathe, one of the most charming love stories which history has given us. On the eighth anniversary of their marriage, the Prince thanks Heaven for having given him "the most beautiful, the best, and the most virtuous of wives." This graceful and romantic side of the Prince's character seemed to me worthy of being shown to the world. If, in presenting this charming idyll to my readers, I can touch some sensitive hearts and inspire them with a little of the sincere admiration which I myself felt for this ideal love story, I shall be fully recompensed for my labour.'

STUDIES IN EARLY VICTORIAN LITERATURE, 1837-1870.

By FREDERIC HARRISON, M.A.,

Author of ' The Choice of Books,' etc.

Large crown 8vo., cloth, 10s. 6d.

CONTENTS.

VICTORIAN LITERATURE.	ANTHONY TROLLOPE.
LORD MACAULAY.	CHARLES DICKENS.
THOMAS CARLYLE.	WILLIAM MAKEPEACE THACKERAY.
BENJAMIN DISRAELI.	CHARLES KINGSLEY.
CHARLOTTE BRONTE.	GEORGE ELIOT.

The essays contained in this volume have already appeared in the *Forum*, but they were written originally on a definite preconceived plan with a view to subsequent publication, and may be taken as an expression of the author's mature literary estimate of the great Victorian writers.

ROBERT LOUIS STEVENSON.

By WALTER RALEIGH, Professor of English Literature at Liverpool University College.

Author of 'The English Novel,' etc.

Crown 8vo., cloth, 2s. 6d.

THE SECRET OF THE DESERT.

By E. D. FAWCETT,
Author of 'Swallowed by an Earthquake,' etc.

With Full-page Illustrations, crown 8vo., cloth, 3s. 6d.

KLEINES HAUSTHEATER.

Fifteen Little Plays in German for Children.

By Mrs. HUGH BELL.

Crown 8vo., cloth, 2s.

Most of these little plays have been adapted from the author's 'Petit Théâtre,' the remainder from a little book of English plays by the same writer entitled 'Nursery Comedies.'

NEW STORY BY THE AUTHOR OF 'MISS BLAKE OF MONKSHALTON.'

ON THE THRESHOLD.

By ISABELLA O. FORD,
Author of 'Miss Blake of Monkshalton.'

One vol., crown 8vo., 3s. 6d.

NEW STORY BY THE AUTHOR OF 'MERRIE ENGLAND.'

TOMMY ATKINS.

A Tale of the Ranks.

By ROBERT BLATCHFORD,

Author of ' A Son of the Forge,' ' Merrie England,' etc.

Crown 8vo., cloth, 6s.

WAGNER'S HEROES.

TANNHAUSER.   PARSIFAL.   HANS SACHS.   LOHENGRIN.

By CONSTANCE MAUD.

Illustrated by H. GRANVILLE FELL.

Crown 8vo., handsomely bound, 5s.

'These are just simple tales about men and women who once really lived on the earth, and about whom the greatest of poet-musicians wrote in that wonderful music-language of his which speaks straight to the heart.   And in this language he told us many things about Parsifal, Lohengrin, Tannhauser, and dear old Hans Sachs, which cannot by any human power be put into words ; but in so far as he did make use of words to explain his marvellous music, I have tried to use the same, and above all never to depart from his idea of the heroes he loved.'—*From the Preface.*

LIFE'S PRESCRIPTION.

In Seven Doses.

By D. MACLAREN MORRISON.

Crown 8vo., parchment, 1s. 6d.

CONTENTS.—1. The Pride of Life.   2. Education.   3. Man.   4. Woman. 5. Marriage.   6. Parents.   7. Home.

A few pages of advice to men and women on the management of their lives ; the reader can hardly fail to be interested in the shrewd and sensible remarks, knowledge of life, sound advice and pleasant anecdote with which the book is enlivened.

CYCLING FOR HEALTH AND PLEASURE.

By L. H. PORTER,

Author of ' Wheels and Wheeling,' etc.

Revised and edited by

F. W. SHORLAND, Amateur Champion 1892-93-94.

With numerous Illustrations, small 8vo., 2s. 6d.

STRENGTH;

Or, The Development and Use of Muscle.

By the Champion, C. A. SAMPSON,

'The strongest man on earth.'

With nearly forty illustrations, 8vo., cloth, 2s. 6d.

TWO NEW COOKERY BOOKS BY COLONEL KENNEY-HERBERT

FIFTY LUNCHES.

FIFTY DINNERS.

By COLONEL A. KENNEY HERBERT,

Author of ' Common-Sense Cookery,' ' Fifty Breakfasts,' etc.

Each vol., crown 8vo., cloth, 2s. 6d.

POULTRY FATTENING.

By EDWARD BROWN,

Author of ' Pleasurable Poultry Keeping,' etc.

With Illustrations, crown 8vo., cloth, 1s. 6d.

NEW BOOKS FOR YOUNG PEOPLE.

PRICE FIVE SHILLINGS EACH.

ERIC THE ARCHER.

By MAURICE HERVEY,
Author of ' The Reef of Gold,' etc.

With numerous Full-page Illustrations, handsomely bound,
crown 8vo., 5s.

DR. GILBERT'S DAUGHTERS.

By MARGARET HARRIET MATHEWS.

Illustrated by CHRIS. HAMMOND.

Crown 8vo., cloth, 5s.

THE FUR SEAL'S TOOTH.

By KIRK MUNROE.

Beautifully Illustrated, crown 8vo., cloth, 5s.

HOW DICK AND MOLLY WENT ROUND THE WORLD.

By M. H. CORNWALL LEGH.

With numerous Illustrations, fcap. 4to., cloth, 5s.

PRICE THREE SHILLINGS AND SIXPENCE EACH.

HUNTERS THREE.

By THOMAS W. KNOX,
Author of ' The Boy Travellers,' etc.

With numerous Illustrations, crown 8vo., cloth, 3s. 6d.

JOEL : A BOY OF GALILEE.

By ANNIE FELLOWS JOHNSTON.

With Ten Full-page Illustrations, crown 8vo., cloth, 3s. 6d.

THE MUSHROOM CAVE.
By EVELYN RAYMOND,
Author of ' The Little Lady of the Horse.'
With Illustrations, crown 8vo., cloth, 3s. 6d.

THE CHILDREN'S HOUR SERIES.

' A pause in the day's occupations
That is known as The Children's Hour.'—LONGFELLOW.

This series will consist of continuous stories for boys and girls from about seven to ten years of age ; great care will be taken by the authors to make the books really interesting to young readers, so that the title of the series may not be misapplied.   Large type will be used, and each volume will be illustrated with several full-page pictures specially drawn for it.

The following volumes are just ready, price Half-a-crown each :

MASTER MAGNUS.
By MRS. E. M. FIELD,
Author of ' Ethne,' ' Little Count Paul,' ' Mixed Pickles,' etc.

With Four Full-page Illustrations, small 8vo., 2s. 6d.

MY DOG PLATO.
By M. H. CORNWALL LEGH,
Author of ' How Dick and Molly went Round the World,' etc.

With Four Full-page Illustrations, small 8vo., 2s. 6d.

Further Volumes are in preparation.

NEW VOLUMES OF
THE CHILDREN'S FAVOURITE SERIES.

PRICE TWO SHILLINGS EACH ; SPECIALLY BOUND, GILT EDGES, 2s. 6d.

MY BOOK OF PERILS.
Exciting stories of adventure and hairbreadth escapes.

MY BOOK OF WONDERS.
An account of some of the most marvellous things in the world described in an interesting way for children.

LONDON : EDWARD ARNOLD, 37 BEDFORD STREET, STRAND, W.C.

Lightning Source UK Ltd.
Milton Keynes UK
UKHW02f1828290318
320258UK00017B/616/P